LIGHTNING

THE POETRY OF RENÉ CHAR

Jean Hugo, frontispiece for *La Fauvette des roseaux* by René Char, courtesy of Pierre-André Benoit.

LIGHTNING
THE POETRY OF RENÉ CHAR

by NANCY KLINE PIORE

NORTHEASTERN UNIVERSITY PRESS
Boston 1981

Editors: Norma Fryatt, Judith Brudnick
Production editor: Deborah Kops
Designer: Catherine Dorin

Piore, Nancy Kline, 1941-
Lightning: the poetry of René Char.

Bibliography: p.   Includes index.

1. Char, René, 1907-   —Criticism and interpretation. I. Title.
PQ2605.H3345Z79   841'.912   80-22001
ISBN 0-930350-08-1
Printed in the United States of America

for POLLY AND SID

CONTENTS

FOREWORD

IN THESE DAYS OF OBSCURE ANALYTIC WRIT-
ings about literature, it is a sheer delight to come upon a readable
synthesis which constructs the essential physiognomy of one of the
most important poets of the twentieth century. René Char passed
through surrealism as did a host of others in the 1925-1940 era.
Being at least a decade younger than the cluster of poets identified
with the movement and a remarkably fertile poet, he surpassed the
label of this coterie and developed quietly but persistently, bringing
to fruition many of the poetic promises made by his predecessors
from Arthur Rimbaud onward.

Professor Nancy Kline Piore acknowledges these antecedents,
but without a rigid study of sources. Instead, she develops thematic
groupings that highlight the poetic aspirations of over a century of
French poets and without categorical assertion, demonstrates that
these have been more completely realized by René Char than by virtually any other contemporary poet.

The hermetic direction proposed by André Breton in the Second
Manifesto, combined with the revolver shot (Breton's oft-quoted
declaration: "The simplest surrealist act consists of going down into
the street, revolver in hand, and shooting at random") has had the
most productive effects on the poetry that survived the haphazard
collages of the run of the mill surrealists. Not enough attention has
been given to the title of *Breton's* second collection of poems: *Le
Revolver à Cheveux Blancs*, which combines the themes of violent
desire with the silvering work of magic of those who probe the
secrets of the universe.

Professor Piore highlights these very paths of exploration in the
works of René Char. With poetic insight, astute observation, and
rich illustrations, she follows the poet in his embrace of the natural

world of bird and tree, in his quest as an attentive hunter, in his sometimes violent venery, in his visions of cosmic fire, meteoric illumination and the combination of explosive and intense brightness characteristic of lightning. Beauty is indeed "convulsive," as Breton commanded that it must be if poetry is to survive.

Professor Piore proves admirably that it has indeed survived in the person and writings of René Char. The obstinate claim, both tender and ferocious, to the importance of being a poet (which we know to have been basic in Guillaume Apollinaire) is brilliantly immanent here.

From Breton on, one can trace a new group of nature poets. Among the most important of these I would judge to be René Char, Jean Mayoux, and Octavio Paz. But there are certainly others not yet identified. The difference between their vision of nature and the pathetic fallacy of the Romantics is that the former presume no sympathy or understanding on the part of nature. Instead, they correlate their own explosive and sensitive forces and project them upon those of natural phenomena in a consortium in which often the mediator is woman.

In the pages of Professor Piore's book we see how this works with René Char. The interweaving of the sacred in the human and the dynamic in nature is carefully delineated. And while there is some overlap in the treatment of sub-topics, it would be virtually impossible to achieve a complete separation of themes in a global poet such as René Char whose vision is unconditionally holistic.

It is a pleasure to welcome a young and promising scholar into the field of poetic criticism whose membership continues to remain sparse though indefatigable. Her book has a clarity that should bring to the appreciation of French poetry new readers who cannot by themselves breach the language barrier; but it should also serve as a valuable, fresh perspective for those who are more familiar with René Char. In bringing his vision and spirit across a cultural frontier, Professor Piore proves herself an unusual intermediary, and American poets and their readers sorely need a model such as René Char.

New York University   Anna Balakian

ACKNOWLEDGMENTS

I WISH TO SALUTE MY "COMPAGNONS DANS LE jardin," all those who have shared Char's poetry with me and lived through the making of this book, most especially Patricia Terry, Anne-Marie Mairesse, Michel Philip, T. Jefferson Kline, Mary Ann Caws; also Alan Cromer, William Frohlich, Judith Brudnick and Deborah Kops. My special thanks to Professor L.C. Breunig who first introduced me to Char's work, and to Professor Frederic Shepler who helped deepen the encounter.

I am obliged to Wellesley College for a travel grant which permitted my visiting the poet in June 1979.

To René Char, who knows that *le poème n'est pas dans le cube*, my most profound gratitude for his repeated welcome, his wit and patience, his poetry.

My grateful acknowledgment to Editions Gallimard for permission to quote from the copyrighted works of René Char: "Congé au vent," "Le météore du 13 août," and fragments from *Fureur et mystère*, © Gallimard, 1949, "Arthur Rimbaud," "Après," and fragments from *Recherche de la base et du sommet*, © Gallimard, 1955, "Complainte du lézard amoureux," "Anoukis et plus tard Jeanne," "Le carreau," and a fragment of "Fête des arbres et du chasseur" from *Les Matinaux* © Gallimard, 1950, "La fauvette des roseaux," "L'une et l'autre," "La route par les sentiers," "L'arbre frappé," "Pourquoi la journée vole," and fragments from *La Parole en archipel*, © Gallimard, 1962, "Effacement du peuplier" and a fragment of "le chien de coeur" from *Le Nu Perdu*, © Gallimard, 1971, "Ebriété" and "Eloquence d'Orion" from *Aromates Chasseurs*, © Gallimard, 1975, "Pour qu'une forêt" from *Commune présence*, © Gallimard, 1964, and fragments from *Chants de la Balandrane*, © Gallimard, 1977, and *Trois coups sous les arbres*, © Gallimard, 1967;

to José Corti for fragments quoted from *Le Marteau sans maître,* ©
José Corti, 1934; to Princeton University Press for "Seuil," "Mon-
tagne déchirée," "Front de la rose," "Réception d'Orion" and
"Feuillet pour la 2e édition du Marteau sans maître, 1945" from
Poems of René Char, translated and annotated by Mary Ann Caws
and Jonathan Griffin © 1976, also " "Le martinet," "L'adolescent
souffleté," "Quatre fascinants," "Le mortel partenaire," "Pour
renouer," "Permanent invisible," "A ***," and fragments from
"La bibliothèque est en feu," "Pour un Prométhée saxifrage," and
"Contre une maison sèche," (translated by Nancy Kline Piore)
reprinted by permission of Princeton University Press; to Random
House for "To Friend-Tree of Counted Days," translated by
William Carlos Williams, and the prose introduction to "The
Meteor of the 13th of August," translated by Jackson Mathews,
from *Hypnos Waking: Poems and Prose by René Char,* © 1956.

LIST OF ABBREVIATIONS:

All quotations are taken from the following volumes, many containing previously published works.

AC   *Aromates chasseurs*. Gallimard, 1975
CB   *Chants de la Balandrane*. Gallimard, 1977
CP   *Commune présence*. Gallimard, 1978
FM   *Fureur et mystère*. Gallimard, collection Poésie, 1967
HW   *Hypnos Waking: Poems and Prose by René Char*, ed. Jackson Mathews. Random House, 1956
LM   *Les Matinaux*. Gallimard, collection Poésie, 1969
LPA   *La Parole en archipel*. Gallimard, collection Poésie, 1969
MSM   *Le Marteau sans maître*. Corti, 1975
NP   *Le Nu perdu*. Gallimard, 1971
NT   *La Nuit talismanique*. Skira, collection Sentiers de la Création, 1972
RBS   *Recherche de la base et du sommet*. Gallimard, collection Poésie, 1971
SP   *Sur la poésie*. GLM, 1974
TCA   *Trois coups sous les arbres*. Gallimard, 1967

A note on the translations: All unmarked translations are the author's. In those instances where she has used the translations of others, the translator's name appears after the English text.

INTRODUCTION

HERE IS A RECENT DIRECTIVE FROM RENÉ CHAR TO himself: "Le souffle levé, descendre à reculons, puis obliquer et suivre le sentier qui ne mène qu'au coeur ensanglanté de soi, source et sépulcre du poème" ["Once the wind has risen, go down backwards, then turn and follow the path which leads only to one's own bloodied heart, source and sepulcher of the poem"] (SP, 33). The wind, the breath of inspiration, swells, to send the poet underground, again, as always, where he will mine from his own bloodied heart the stuff of poetry. His image recalls the aging Yeats's "foul rag–and–bone shop of the heart."[1] But never do we have the sense that René Char has lost his ladder, nor, if he had, that he would lie down in his poem's sepulcher. Char's Poet never lies down, not even in dying (see "Éloquence d'Orion" ["Orion's Eloquence"], (AC, 43). Rather, having followed the oblique path to his heart, he will now turn and climb back up, into the upper air, to shape his raw materials, until—refined, compressed, *impersonalized*—they form a poem: "Le dessein de la poésie étant de nous rendre souverain en nous impersonnalisant, nous touchons, grâce au poème, à la plénitude de ce qui n'était qu'esquissé ou déformé par les vantardises de l'individu" ["Poetry's purpose being to make us supreme by impersonalizing us, thanks to the poem we touch upon the plenitude of that which was at best sketched-out or deformed by the boastings of the individual"] (LPA, 116).

The poems of René Char, whether they be fragmentary in form or structured as prose poems, strike us by the terseness of their beauty and by the wholly elusive presence of their maker, visible only in his invisibility. He resembles his trout, whose absence pervades the poem named for her, or his meteor, seen in its dying as a luminous line across the sky. On the page it is the poet's disappearance that illuminates. He writes: "Un poète doit laisser des traces de son passage, non des preuves. Seules les traces font rêver" ["A poet must leave traces of his passage, not proofs. Only traces make us dream"] (LPA, 153). His characteristic gesture is departure, or in terms of writing, ellipsis—first, at the juncture between life and art (virtually every poem has a "story," Char says, but the reader is not privy to it, it gets left out, or transformed beyond recognition, although the poet frequently leaves in just enough autobiography to tantalize us, as in "Anoukis et plus tard Jeanne" ["Anoukis and Later Jeanne"]); second, at the level of language itself (he is the most elliptical of poets). This double ellipsis gives to everything he writes its distinctive and compelling mystery. His is hardly confessional poetry, yet like the spider to whom he compares himself, he spins from his own center and from the center of his life, and all his work glimmers with the tension between disclosure and concealment, what the poet shows and what he hides on the page. The reader feels, as Helen Vendler has remarked, that "he writes with absolute candor, but in a secret language."[2] A language, it must be added, that can be learned. Surely this is central to the experience of reading René Char, this sense that one has come upon a poetic universe that is by turns transparent and completely opaque—of a beautiful opacity—but where at any given moment an illumination may occur, a connection be made, so that the mystery which was felt to be unsolvable but full of meaning yields its meaning to us, opens to us like a door, a book, a lover, and we are admitted into places where we could not go before, our pleasure, our delight akin to Char's, perhaps, in the moment when he forged the image.

The following pages offer one reader's understanding of certain portions of this mysterious poetic universe and explore the issue of artistic exposure—how much the poet allows his reader to see—as it relates to Char's major themes and images, to his political stance, to the chief players in his poetry, and to his poetic technique itself. My approach has not been chronological, but rather through imagery.

Let us begin with a few biographical facts. René Char was born in L'Isle-sur-Sorgue, in 1907.[3] He lives there still, and his poetry takes its fragrance, its intense light, its creatures, from the Vaucluse, a water landscape ringed with mountains, and filtered on the page through the immense dark imagination of the poet. The early death of his father and the communal tragedies of this century cast deep shadows across his poetry, whose characteristic hour has always been the dawn, but a red dawn. (The color is not unambiguous. And then too, dawn is born of Night's blackness.) World War I occurred in the middle of Char's childhood; World War II in the middle of his manhood, and he was an active participant in the Resistance. The wreckage of the world, as he testifies with anguish, has continued ever since. But so, in counterpoint to it, has the poet's love of the earth and his attempt to salvage it, its beauty and fragility. And if certain themes such as warfare and eroticism have diminished in his later work, this theme—a passion for the planet and for the creatures who inhabit it—has only been strengthened, so that in 1975 he published a book called *Aromates chasseurs* [*Aromatic Hunters*], whose hero Orion leaves the sky to come back down among us, a human meteor who has the earth—no longer the moon—for honey (AC, 27).

In the figure of Orion and the voyage that he undertakes the two spheres of Char's poetic universe, the celestial and the terrestrial, are joined. Orion is a bridge-builder, as the poet suggests in texts like "Pontonniers" ["Pontoniers"] and "Orion Iroquois." But he is also a cluster of stars and a solitary, blinded hunter—which makes of him the quintessential Charian hero. For, as we shall see in the following pages, the night sky, the Night itself, and the activity of hunting are among Char's recurrent leitmotifs; all are connected with love-making and with the making of poetry; and the hunter-lover-poet's power of sight (or lack of it) is crucial, as is the balance he chooses to strike between his solitude and his sense of community.

The tension between these last two—separateness and "common presence"—has been as great in the poet's personal life as in his work. He himself is a deeply private man, a man of silence, to use his own phrase, yet he participated actively in two of the most important communal efforts of the century, Surrealism and the Resistance, and both have marked his work.

He came to Surrealism late, in terms of the movement (1929-1930) and was a decade younger than his colleagues Eluard and Breton, with whom he collaborated on one book, *Ralentir travaux* [Slacken Labors].[4] He was already published at that time, and it was when he sent his second book of poems to Eluard that the older poet came south to meet him. Char moved to Paris then, into the thick of things, returning to live in the Vaucluse only in 1934. In that same year he published *Le marteau sans maître* [*The Hammer with No Master*], his most important pre-World War II collection. In the following year he broke formally, though without venom, with the Surrealist movement.

There is some critical debate as to just how bona fide a Surrealist Char was.[5] He never practiced automatic writing, and his poetry is characterized by quite the opposite of the verbal flux we associate with Breton, for example. (Char writes: "Le poète se remarque à la quantité de pages insignifiantes qu'il n'écrit pas. Il a toutes les rues de la vie oublieuse pour distribuer ses moyennes aumônes et cracher le petit sang dont il ne meurt pas" ["You can tell a poet by the number of insignificant pages he does not write. He can use all the streets of forgetful life to distribute his unremarkable alms and spit up the minor blood that doesn't kill him"] (RBS, 164). Char's imagery has always been deeply reasoned, *wrought*, and his style always highly elliptical. Charian images do not float haphazardly into view, the poet goes after them with a pick and hammer; they are mined by him, underground: "Demain commenceront les travaux poétiques / Précédés du cycle de la mort volontaire / Le règne de l'obscurité a coulé la raison le diamant dans la mine" ["Tomorrow poetic labors will begin / Preceded by the cycle of voluntary death. / Obscurity's reign has poured out reason, the diamond in the mine"] (MSM, 75). If his raw materials come out of the unconscious, this alone does not validate them for Char. They must be shaped by the poet's consciousness. His discourse, like his serenity, is *clenched*.

What he does share with Surrealist doctrine is an emphasis on the marvelous in everyday life and an openness to those rare, privileged instants when all the disparate elements of reality come together in illuminative synthesis, "cet instant où la beauté, après s'être longtemps fait attendre surgit des choses communes, traverse notre champ radieux, lie tout ce qui peut être lié, allume tout ce qui doit être allumé de notre gerbe de ténèbres" ["that instant when beauty, so long awaited, rises out of common things, crosses our radiant field of vision, binds together all that can be bound, lights all that must be lit in our sheaf of shadows"] (RBS, 170). His is a poetry of the sudden encounter—between lovers, adversaries, hunters and their prey, the poet and poetry, the reader and the poem; between words themselves within the text, within the image. And these encounters do not leave their participants unchanged. They are explosive fusions that destroy the elements fused to create new unities. "Il y a des destructions nécessaires" ["There are necessary destructions"], wrote Rimbaud. "Enfin si tu détruis, que ce soit avec des outils nuptiaux" ["If you destroy, then may it be with nuptial tools"], writes Char (LM, 81). He is a poet who exalts life, communication, beauty, the world of nature. But he is also a Heraclitean poet, deeply pessimistic, who sees the universe in terms of opposites colliding, fire, constant flux, and violent metamorphosis.

Particularly as it applies to his conception of poetry, Char's passionate, combative stance constitutes another link between him and the Surrealists, with whom he shares a sense of poetry as rebellion, desperate, revolutionary, and fertile; and a belief that art, man's most precious radium and most effective weapon, can transform him and the quality of his life. Still, the creation of art, no matter how revolutionary, how *committed*, requires an essential solitude: "La poésie est la solitude. . .qui a le moyen de se confier; on n'est, à l'aube, l'ennemi d'aucun, excepté des bourreaux" ("Poetry is solitude. . .which has found the way to be confiding; at dawn one isn't the enemy of anyone, except the hangman"] (RBS, 150). The poet's withdrawal from the Surrealist community was inevitable. But their brief association had strengthened him and had served as a kind of basic training, or boot camp, for the Maquis. As Dominique Fourcade suggests, "the Surrealists must have confirmed in him the belief that there existed in life a small society of sensitive beings, totally isolated from society at large and in violent opposition to it; in the bosom of that small society, Char could go into action."[6]

Four years after his rift with Surrealism, war broke out. The poet was mobilized and sent to Alsace, where he saw France fall; he then returned to Provence to fight in the Resistance, his nom de guerre: le capitaine Alexandre.

His years in the Maquis left an indelible imprint on Char's poetry (not to say his life). As I have tried to indicate, the war experience seems to have been anticipated, to a certain extent, by the Surrealist experience, its emphasis on community and revolt, violence and the unexpected. But the essence of art is play, if deeply serious play, and poems take place in the heart and on the page. This fact in no way diminishes their power. Quite the contrary: "La poésie est à la fois parole et provocation silencieuse, désespérée de notre être-exigeant pour la venue d'une réalité qui sera sans concurrente. Imputrescible celle-là. Impérissable, non, car elle court les dangers de tous. Mais la seule qui visiblement triomphe de la mort matérielle. . . ." ["Poetry is simultaneously word and silent desperate provocation on the part of our exacting-being, aimed at the coming of a peerless reality, incorruptible. Not imperishable, for it runs the same dangers as everyone. But the only reality that visibly triumphs over material death"] (LPA, 197). This empowers poetry—alone—to "steal" the poet's death from him (LPA, 147). However, he himself continues to exist in the flesh and in the world as well; and to write poetry, even if the poet calls it resistance, is a different endeavor from actively participating in the Resistance. During the war years, what had been metaphor became reality, both around the poet and within him.

After the war, in 1945, he wrote:

Vers quelle mer enragée, ignorée même des poètes, pouvait bien s'en aller, aux environs de 1930, ce fleuve mal aperçu qui coulait dans des terres où les accords de la fertilité déjà se mouraient, où l'allégorie de l'horreur commençait à se concrétiser, ce fleuve radiant et énigmatique baptisé MARTEAU SANS MAITRE? Vers l'hallucinante expérience de l'homme noué au Mal, de l'homme massacré et pourtant victorieux.

La clef du MARTEAU SANS MAITRE tourne dans la réalité pressentie des années 1937-1944. Le premier rayon qu'elle délivre hésite entre l'imprécation du supplice et le magnifique amour. (Feuillet pour la 2e édition, 1945) [MSM, 13]

Toward what enraged sea, unknown even to poets, could this river, scarcely even perceived, have been flowing, around 1930, coursing through lands where the covenants of fertility were already expiring, where the allegory of horror was beginning to take on concrete existence—this radiant and enigmatic river baptized *The Hammer with No Master?* Toward the hallucinating experience of man riveted to evil, of man massacred and still victorious.

The key of *The Hammer with No Master* turns in the reality of the years 1937-1944, foreshadowed. The first ray it gives forth hesitates between the imprecation of agony and a magnificent love. (Preface for second edition, 1945)

Mary Ann Caws

It will be remembered that *Le marteau sans maître* was first published in 1934. In it, according to the poet, the war which did not erupt till five years later was already present. Certainly Char's own native violence, a violence pre-dating his association with Surrealism (the book he sent to Eluard in 1929 was entitled *Arsenal*), his thirst for justice, his anger and desire, his need to do battle for that which breaks easily, the very values and ways of thinking that drew him into the underground, had already begun to be articulated on the page. He had already spoken of poetry as warfare, as endless combat and voluntary death, within the context of a poem called "Commune présence" ["Common Presence"] which ended *Le marteau sans maître*. The Resistance made of the poet an actual guerrilla soldier, and validated the metaphor. I do not think the importance of this intersection between life and art can be too greatly stressed.

Proust has written of it, of the anticipatory nature of art and of the interface between text and the daily living of the artist:

> . . . we do not sufficiently reflect that the life of the writer does not come to an end with [a] particular work, that the same nature which caused him to have certain sufferings, and which then entered his work, will continue to live after the work has been concluded. . . . His life will resemble his work and in future the poet will scarcely need to write, for he will be able to find in what he has already written the anticipatory outline of what will then be happening.[7]

Char is a more political creature than Proust, and his sufferings arise as much from the world around him as from the world within him. But Proust's statement still applies, as does Char's own: "Il advient au poète d'échouer au cours de ses recherches sur un rivage où il n'était attendu que beaucoup plus tard. . ." ["It sometimes happens that the poet runs aground, in the course of his search, on a riverbank where he was not expected until much later"] (SP, 8).

The war years seem to have influenced his work in at least two ways: on one level, by tempering his attitude toward human beings and the voice with which he speaks of them, so that his early anger and revolt are counterbalanced now with tenderness and deep fraternity; on another level, by reinforcing his conception of poetry as guerrilla warfare and his sense of himself as a *Résistant*.[8]

After the war Char leaves the underground to move back out onto the page, but strengthened in the need to keep himself half-hidden in the very moment when he is most present. Ellipsis and fragmentation characterize his work. The poem is defined as veil and revelation, simultaneously: "Tu es reposoir d'obscurité sur ma face trop offerte, poème" ["You are, poem, a wayside altar of darkness on my too-exposed face"] (LPA, 134). The poet has put aside his gun and taken up his words again as weapons, but since he is both hunted and hunter, and since in the poetic universe that he creates, as in the world of the Maquis, to be caught is to be killed, his words must also serve as shelter, as a hiding place. Were we to try to characterize the particular quality of Char's poetic voice and of his greatness, we would focus on this paradox: his is not simply lyric but also political poetry. It repeatedly addresses such questions as freedom versus oppression, truth versus lies; it is direct, directed to us; yet it eludes us at the same time. *Engagé* and *hermétique*, committed yet mysterious, Char's poetry—like the creatures it evokes—retains an essential distance. "Supprimer l'éloignement tue," he writes. "Les dieux ne meurent que d'être parmi nous" ["Doing away with distance kills. The gods die only from being amongst us"] (RBS, 183). His poetic universe is permeated by violence and by enduring invisibility, and his lark and snake and swift reflect their maker and embody the ellipsis at the center of his work as they flash in and out of hiding on the page. The lightning bolt and meteor participate in Char's "guérilla sans reproche" ["blameless guerrilla warfare"] as does the rose, the lightning's earthly feminine counterpart, as ephemeral and as dazzling as itself: "Eclair et rose, en nous, dans leur fugacité, pour nous accomplir, s'ajoutent" ["Within us, lightning bolt and rose in their transience, to complete us, join"] (LM, 152).

Let us look at the poems. First, the earth poems, especially Char's bestiary and the melancholy hunter who comes to disturb it. Then the sky poems, as they reflect and complement the earth. And finally those dealing specifically with the poet himself and with his love, the woman Poetry.

CHAPTER 1
BIRD AND TREE

Une ingérence innommable a ôté aux choses,
aux circonstances, aux êtres, leur hasard d'auréole.
Il n'y a d'avènement pour nous qu'à partir de cette auréole.
Elle n'immunise pas. [LPA, 204]

An unspeakable meddling has stripped things,
circumstances, beings of their adventitious halo.
There can be no advent for us without that halo.
It does not immunize.

ONE OF THE EARLIEST AND MOST INTENSE EN-
counters in Char's poetic universe is entirely olfactory. It occurs in a
windless instant, in the absence of speech, in a place far distant from
the flowers whose fragrance, rendered by the poet as light, haloes
the text and the girl who passes through it, her back turned toward
the setting sun, her lips bearing a trace (perhaps) of Night's humid-
ity. It would be sacrilege to speak to her, writes Char. He tells
us—and himself—to step back away from her, to let her go:

CONGÉ AU VENT

A flancs de coteau du village bivouaquent des champs
fournis de mimosas. A l'époque de la cueillette, il arrive que,
loin de leur endroit, on fasse la rencontre extrêmement
odorante d'une fille dont les bras se sont occupés durant la
journée aux fragiles branches. Pareille à une lampe dont
l'auréole de clarté serait de parfum, elle s'en va, le dos tourné
au soleil couchant.
Il serait sacrilège de lui adresser la parole.
L'espadrille foulant l'herbe, cédez-lui le pas du chemin.
Peut-être aurez-vous la chance de distinguer sur ses lèvres la
chimère de l'humidité de la Nuit? [FM, 20]

————

IN THE ABSENCE OF WIND

On flanks of the village hillside bivouac fields that are
deep in mimosa. Far away from the harvest of the flowers,
you may come very fragrantly face to face with a girl whose
arms have been occupied all day long in the fragile branches.
Like a lamp whose halo of brightness would be a perfume,
she goes her way, her back to the setting sun.

It would be sacrilege to speak to her.
Your sandals crushing the grass, yield her the path.
Won't you, perhaps, have the luck to perceive on her lips a
shimmer of humid Night?

Patricia Terry

Let her go, the poet says. How could we do otherwise? She
exists as a scent, and as a scent she is penetrating, we are
defenseless: "Nulle grille qui s'oppose" ["No gate to make opposition"] (LPA, 123); but she cannot be captured either. She can be
breathed, not touched, not even seen—except at one remove, in the
Baudelairian simile which makes of her a lamp whose nimbus of
light might be perfume. Her beauty and elusiveness, the poet's
desire and his gesture of relinquishment, lie at the heart of the
Charian encounter, at the very heart of Char's poetry.

In a later text, "Les compagnons dans le jardin" ["Companions
in the Garden"], he writes: "Les oiseaux libres ne souffrent pas
qu'on les regarde. Demeurons obscurs, renonçons à nous, près
d'eux" ["Free birds refuse to be looked at. Let us stay in the
shadows, relinquish ourselves, close to them"]. And the adjuration
is immediately followed by this verse, the poem's last: "O survie encore, toujours meilleure!" ["Another survival, always better!"]
(LPA, 154). What assures survival here—of friendship, passion,
poetry—as it did in "Congé au vent," is a chosen distance, defined
this time as obscurity. Once again, we are urged to relinquish a contact that might impinge on the freedom of the other, but whereas
that contact was verbal in "Congé au vent" ("Say nothing!") now it
is defined as visual. We must not even look at one another, we must
elect invisibility, our model: free birds.

Virtually all of the animals in Char's poetry are hunted by men,
but birds are the prey of predilection—"Oiseaux que nous lapidons
au pur moment de votre véhémence. . ." ["Birds we lapidate in the
pure moment of your vehemence. . ."] (RBS, 171). A notable exception to this rule is the eagle, the poet's own "rival hunter" (LM, 51).
He is regal though, he lives at the top of the mountain, and most of
the poet's winged creatures do not share his size, his distance. They
are fragile, fleeting, and much too close to the world of men:

LA FAUVETTE DES ROSEAUX

L'arbre le plus exposé à l'oeil du fusil n'est pas un arbre
pour son aile. La remuante est prévenue: elle se fera muette
en le traversant. La perche de saule happée est à l'instant
cédée par l'ongle de la fugitive. Mais dans la touffe de

roseaux où elle amerrit, quelles cavatines! C'est ici qu'elle
chante. Le monde entier le sait.

Eté, rivière, espaces, amants dissimulés, toute une lune
d'eau, la fauvette répète: "Libre, libre, libre, libre. . ." [LPA,
160]

THE WARBLER IN THE REEDS

The tree most exposed to the shotgun's eye is not a tree
for her wing. The quicksilver one is forewarned: she will pass
through in silence. Her fugitive claw grapples and gives up at
once a perch in the willow. But from her landing place in the
clustered reeds, what cavatinas! It is here that she sings. As
the whole world knows.

Summer, the river, spaces, lovers hidden away, a whole
watermoon, the warbler repeats, "Free, free, free, free. . ."

Patricia Terry

In this transparent poem, as delicate as the creature it captures—but does not kill—the warbler remains mute until she is invisible. She must. She must not call attention to herself, for what is
on the lookout in her poem is the eye of the gun, and to be seen is to
be shot. She will refrain from song, then, while she passes by the
most exposed tree. Barely touching it, she is pure movement,
noiseless flight, until by the end of her bumpy third sentence she has
disappeared. Another Charian departure. We do not see her land,
however briefly, on the tree branch; we see her let go. And up to this
point, she has not even been named: she is "la remuante" and "la
fugitive," her whole identity consisting in her flight from exposure.
Even when she is present, she is only partially present: her wing and
her talon are all that appear on the page. The poet's synecdoche and
ellipsis protect her from the reader, just as her own speed and
silence protect her from the hunter's gun.

Prior to her disappearance into the reeds, there is only one active verb and that is in the future tense: "elle se fera muette"; and
the effect of the poem's passive verb forms is to underline the fixed
quality of the landscape. In contrast to the moving bird, gun and
willow tree (which constitutes a fatal trap for her) are absolutely
static. One feels the setting for her death to be eternal. She flees
across its unchanging face, Char's use of past participles
strengthening the impression that her journey is so fast it is over
before we even notice it. We are aware of her flight before and after

she makes it. But once she has arrived in the clustered reeds, all the verbs turn active. Hidden now, invisible, the warbler is safe to sing her joyous cavatina and the poet to call her by her name: "Eté, rivière, espaces, amants dissimulés, toute une lune d'eau, la fauvette répète: 'Libre, libre, libre, libre. . . .' "

The message of the warbler's lyric is liberty, and she, who is not free to leave her hiding place, escapes it as song. Just as the poet, like her a prisoner, creates his own illusory freedom with language. Neither of them is truly free. The gun is always out there, waiting. They are both what Char calls "freedom-givers," she to the natural world, he to the human world, whose voice they each, respectively, become: but "le donneur de liberté n'est libre que dans les autres. Le poète ne jouit que de la liberté des autres" ["The freedom-giver is only free in others. The poet enjoys only the freedom of others"] (RBS, 132).

Still, something curious happens to the syntax at the end of the warbler's poem, which considerably expands her freedom—which constitutes, in a sense, her liberation. In the final sentence of the text a characteristically Charian ellipsis occurs. The mediating term, "le modalisateur," as Gérard Genette would call it,[1] has been left out between the bird and all those phenomena named by the poet before her, and which, on a first reading, seem to be simply the enumerated parts of the "entire world" that is listening to her sing. In fact, Char has placed all these phenomena *in apposition* to her, so that the warbler *becomes* summer, river, spaces, secretive lovers, a whole watermoon, and they become her. Syntactically, the identification between them is complete, and thus, not only do these phenomena participate directly in her song, but she participates directly in their freedom.

This is considerable. For summer is the most open of seasons, and the moving river a major image of liberty and revolt for Char, who still lives a stone's throw from the Sorgue, "Rivière au coeur jamais détruit dans ce monde fou de prison" ["River whose heart is never destroyed in this world crazy for prison"] (FM, 211). Space, plural in the warbler's poem, multiple, is associated with the two great liberating adventures, love and poetry. And here are the lovers, hidden like the bird, threatened like her in their fragility, but in the amorous instant and in her song, free. And then the mysterious image, "toute une lune d'eau." Literally, "lune d'eau" is a white water lily. But the poet has placed his water lily in a temporal expression, "toute une. . ." So that, especially in its juxtaposition with the lovers in the poem, Char's white water lily suggests a transmuted "lune de miel" (honeymoon) and becomes a designation of time—the warbler sings for "a whole watermoon"—as well as a visual image. The bird perches at the base of the reeds, near the water's surface, and all that surface is reflected light and petals as white and luminous as the moon. Thus, at the end of the poem, all heaviness evaporates, all things are transformed and unified, freed of their earthbound substance to become pure light, pure song, freed of their separate and constraining identities to become transparence.

The operative verb here is "to free." We have seen that the warbler is, on one level, a symbol for the poet and that her text speaks to the problem of artistic exposure: the bird must hide before she sings or she will be destroyed. The poet must disappear within his text, for his own sake—it is too dangerous to be fully seen—but also for ours.

"Qui délivrera le message n'aura pas d'identité," writes Char. "Il n'oppressera pas" ["He who delivers the message will have no identity. He will not oppress"] (AC, 10). The poet, like the warbler, is a political bird, a "donneur de liberté" in the largest sense of the term, and in each poem he will enter into what Maurice Blanchot has called "that responsibility of the word which speaks without exercising any form of power."[2] He will efface himself, to leave us free. Like La Liberté as she first appears after the Occupation, he will come "par cette ligne blanche. . .cygne sur la blessure" ["by this white line. . .a swan on the wound"] (FM, 52). Restrained, curative, barely visible; his every song a gesture of resistance and a piece of pure freedom, of "désir demeuré désir" ["desire which has remained desire"] (FM, 73). However, the liberating transparence which he and his warbler offer us at the end of her poem and which may be found in many of his most beautiful texts (see "Le Thor" [FM, 159] for example) is always threatened by the hovering dark: death as it menaces the individual, oppression as it menaces the race. These are the enemies Char never loses sight of.

He writes: "Nous n'avons qu'une ressource avec la mort: faire de l'art avant elle" ["We have but one resource with death: to make art before it"] (LPA, 202). But what of oppression? Poetry is one answer. But poetry, the Surrealists notwithstanding, is essentially an individual act, and an intellectual one. On a pragmatic political level, common presence—collective action—is another, and even in so seemingly unpolitical a text as the one we have been looking at, the collective is evoked, not simply in the warbler's final merging with the world around her (which occurs in that moment when she makes her art), but also in the earlier image of the tuft of reeds (which shelter the artist). It will be remembered that she shuns the solitary willow, for it represents exposure to the enemy. Only when she has alighted amid the "touffe de roseaux," in the clustered vegetable community, is she safe—if tenuously, for the reeds are as fragile as she, and as the rest of us. The poet writes elsewhere: "Oiseaux qui confiez votre gracilité, votre sommeil périlleux à un ramas de roseaux, le froid venu, comme nous vous ressemblons!" ["Birds who, once the cold has come, entrust your slenderness, your perilous sleep to a handful of reeds—how alike we are!"](LPA, 148).

The collective aspect of these Pascalian plants and their protective function in Char's universe, as well as their analogy with the human condition, is even clearer in the following poem. Here the protagonist is not a bird, but an equally tender creature, an adolescent boy, his growing up seen as movement out of solitude into the community of men:

L'ADOLESCENT SOUFFLETÉ

Les mêmes coups qui l'envoyaient au sol le lançaient en même temps loin devant sa vie, vers les futures années où, quand il saignerait, ce ne serait plus à cause de l'iniquité d'un seul. Tel l'arbuste que réconfortent ses racines et qui presse ses rameaux meurtris contre son fût résistant, il descendait ensuite à reculons dans le mutisme de ce savoir et dans son innocence. Enfin il s'échappait, s'enfuyait et devenait souverainement heureux. Il atteignait la prairie et la barrière des roseaux dont il cajolait la vase et percevait le sec frémissement. Il semblait que ce que la terre avait produit de plus noble et de plus persévérant, l'avait, en compensation, adopté.

Il recommencerait ainsi jusqu'au moment où, la nécessité de rompre disparue, il se tiendrait droit et attentif parmi les hommes, à la fois plus vulnérable et plus fort. [LM, 58]

THE ADOLESCENT SLAPPED

The very blows that sent him to the ground also flung him far ahead of his life, toward future years when what caused him to bleed would no longer be the injustice of one person alone. Then, like a bush taking comfort in its roots and pressing its bruised branches against a resistant bole, he went down backwards into the muteness of this knowledge and his innocence. Finally he fled, escaped, to become supremely happy. He reached the meadow and the barrier of reeds, whose mud he cajoled, perceiving their dry quivering. It seemed that earth's most noble and most perseverant offspring had, in compensation, adopted him.

In this way he would begin again, until the moment when, no longer having to be separate, he would stay, to hold himself straight and attentive among men, more vulnerable yet stronger.

The structure of the text is remarkably similar to that of "The Warbler in the Reeds." Both open with human violence, or its threat, and describe the withdrawal and muteness of the protagonist as he or she takes flight, ultimately to be adopted by the earth, by the natural community, the meadow and the reeds. The adolescent, like the warbler, is supremely happy as soon as he escapes, though he does not express his happiness and solidarity as song. Rather, he makes of the reeds his playmates, their dry quivering analogous to his own. And whereas the bird's fragility and need to make herself invisible are permanent, this is not so of the reed-child, who will become a man and one day shed the need to run from his tormentors. Carrying within him always the mark of his adoptive parents, when he steps forward to confront iniquity he will hold himself like a reed, "droit et attentif. . .plus vulnérable et plus fort." More vulnerable because he has come out of hiding and committed himself to the human community, stronger for exactly the same reason. Just as the reeds collectively form a barrier against the wind (which they do all over the Vaucluse, where they are erected to shelter young crops), so men collectively represent a barrier against the forces of evil. But to confront these forces, even in the company of one's comrades, is to put oneself at deepest peril. And then too, for the natural recluse, common presence is not easy, nor can it be experienced without ambivalence.

Char does not mention the Maquis in this poem, just as he does not mention Pascal, but both are present. It seems to me no more plausible that a former Maquisard might speak of "resistant" plants without thinking of the former,[3] than it is that a modern French poet could write of reeds and men without calling up echoes of Mallarmé's faun and of Pascal. The presence of the latter becomes explicit in the following wartime text, dated 1945. Here is the last paragraph in Char's description of his clandestine departure from France for North Africa, where he was to serve as liaison between the invading Allies and the Resistance forces in the Midi:

> Il ne devait pas dépendre, hélas, de mes moyens qu'une ferveur de la première aurore trouvât des interlocuteurs dignes d'elle, ni que sa beauté farouche fût comprise et sauvegardée. L'homme battu mais invincible, périodiquement couché et foulé par la meute, restera-t-il toujours le roseau d'*avant* Pascal? [RBS, 24. Char's italics]
>
> ---
>
> Alas, why must it depend on my feeble means that the fervor of first dawn find spokesmen worthy of it, or that its ferocious beauty be understood and safeguarded. Man beaten but invincible, periodically struck down and trampled by the crowd—will he always remain the reed *before* Pascal?

He would not have us be unthinking reeds, and if his poetry is provocation, guerrilla warfare, one of its objectives is to rouse us, to arouse us, so that the fervor of the early dawn, the primal dawn, its ferocious beauty, will not be allowed to perish—by us, mankind, beaten yet invincible, trampled periodically by the pack; forever *unthinking?* The poet's question is a bitter one, written in a bitter time, and it reflects once again his ambivalent feelings toward his fellow creatures. If the warbler in the reeds and the wounded adolescent express Char's own ephemerality and passion, they also share with him a deep ambivalence toward men, who carry guns, after all, both real and metaphorical, and shoot each other as well as birds.

The poet and his hunted creatures are alike, too, in the ramparts they construct—of twigs. They flee into invisibility. And paired with visual eclipse is muteness. We began this chapter with "Congé au vent," a text in which silence preserves what is sacred and speech is equated with sacrilege. We then saw that the warbler, in order to avoid her own death, could not sing until she was invisible. In "L'Adolescent souffleté," the blows the boy receives project him "far ahead of his life," send him reeling into his own future, into an age when it will no longer be the iniquity of a single individual that causes him to bleed. The boy understands what has happened, but wordlessly, and he withdraws into "the muteness of this knowledge" and into his innocence. Only afterwards does he run.

Silence, then, is directly connected with wholeness. It keeps the individual and the individual moment intact. Words break things.

This is complicated for a poet. But if he had any doubts, the Occupation dispelled them. Once again metaphor and reality mirror one another, match, and *Fureur et mystère*, the postwar collection which contains, among other texts, "Congé au vent" and Char's fragmentary wartime journal "Feuillets d'Hypnos" ["Leaves of Hypnos"], bears witness to their confluence. Muteness is one of its recurrent themes.

For the poet, Char tells us, to be mute under Nazi rule was an act of self-denial and resistance and carried with it a concurrent commitment to action:

> Certaines époques de la condition de l'homme subissent l'assaut glacé d'un mal qui prend appui sur les points les plus déshonorés de la nature humaine. Au centre de cet ouragan, le poète complètera par le refus de soi le sens de son message, puis se joindra au parti de ceux qui, ayant ôté à la souffrance son masque de légitimité, assurent le retour éternel de l'entêté portefaix, passeur de justice. [FM, 79]

> Certain eras in the human condition undergo the chilling assault of an evil which finds support in the most dishonored parts of human nature. At the center of this hurricane, the poet will complete the meaning of his message by self-denial, subsequently joining with those who, having stripped suffering of its mask of legitimacy, assure the eternal return of the stubborn porter who ferries back justice.

In another text entitled "Song of Refusal" and subtitled "Beginning of the Partisan," he describes his temporary, painful silence in the following terms: "Le poète est retourné pour de longues années dans le néant du père. Ne l'appelez pas, vous tous qui l'aimez. S'il vous semble que l'aile de l'hirondelle n'a plus de miroir sur terre, oubliez ce bonheur." ["The poet has returned for long years into the nothingness of the father. Do not call him, all you who love him. If it seems to you that the swallow's wing no longer has an earthly mirror, forget that happiness."] (FM, 48). It is like dying, the worst of exiles, no longer to practice poetry, no longer to mirror the swallow.

Jean Starobinski has commented on the dual nature of Char's wartime muteness. Necessitated, on the one hand, by his very real duties elsewhere (Char notes, "J'écris brièvement. Je ne puis guère *m'absenter* longtemps." ["I write briefly. I can scarcely *absent myself* for long."] [FM, 94; Char's italics]), it would have been inappropriate, in any case, Starobinski suggests, for the poet to sing at the top of his lungs: "Muteness alone, at this moment, is capable of giving the accurate measure of hope; muteness or those notes akin to silence, which speak of waiting and watching in the shadows."[4]

During the war the poet's compatriots, as well, remain mute, and although there are times when "les yeux seuls sont encore capables de pousser un cri" ["only the eyes are capable of crying out"] (FM, 112), most often to keep silent is an act of defiance. It takes courage, is in fact synonymous with courage: "Nous n'appartenons à personne sinon au point d'or de cette lampe inconnue de nous, inaccessible à nous qui tient éveillés le courage et le silence" ["We belong to no one if not to the golden point of that lamp, unknown to us, inaccessible to us, which keeps awake courage and silence"] (FM, 87). To refuse to speak despite torture and terror, in order to protect one's comrades, represents the most courageous form of solidarity.

In "Feuillets d'Hypnos," Char describes the day the Nazis came looking for him in a small village where he was hiding out. While they terrorized the populace and beat one young man in particular, the poet waited, hidden in an empty house. He cannot see the beating, but hears the blows and insults: "A voice leaned screaming over the swollen body: 'Where is he? Take us.' Followed by silence. And kicks and rifle butts rained down. . .I estimated that the poor fellow would be quiet for five more minutes, then, inevitably, he *would talk*." Instead, the SS are suddenly inundated, awash in crowds of villagers—old people, women, and children—who arrive "according to an *organized plan*; hurrying without haste, literally streaming over the SS, paralyzing them, 'with the best of intentions.' " Unable to continue their interrogation, the Nazis leave in a rage. And then, but only then, "with infinite prudence. . .eyes, anxious and good, looked in my direction, like a stream of light passed over my window." This act of solidarity, which takes the form of silence, calls forth a deep response from the partisan-poet: "I loved my fellow men ferociously that day, far beyond the sacrifice" (FM, 119–120; Char's italics).

Clearly, the warbler in the reeds lives a similar adventure in her poem, written and published long years after the war (in *La parole en archipel* [*The Word as Archipelago*], 1960). The ex-Maquisard has not forgotten. Invisibility and muteness, coupled with common presence, saved him from the eye of the gun. His warbler resorts to the same defenses, and her relationship to nature is as reciprocal as the guerrilla's relationship to the villagers. He is fighting for their freedom; they shelter him. She takes shelter in the reeds, shaking off her solitude to sing, and so create, the freedom of the whole natural world. "Accumule, puis distribue," Char instructs himself in "Feuillets": "Sois la partie du miroir de l'univers la plus dense, la plus utile et la moins apparente" ["Gather in, then distribute. Be the most dense, most useful and least apparent part of the mirror of the universe"] (FM, 127).

Like the poet, the warbler is a hidden mirror to the universe, and so is another Charian creature, the lizard in love, a tenant of the camouflaging stone, who serves as lookout for the threatened goldfinch. Part of the lizard's "Complaint" goes as follows:

N'égraine pas le tournesol,
Tes cyprès auraient de la peine,
Chardonneret, reprends ton vol
Et reviens à ton nid de laine. . .

L'homme fusille, cache-toi;
Le tournesol est son complice.
Seules les herbes sont pour toi,
Les herbes des champs qui se plissent.

Le serpent ne te connaît pas,
Et la sauterelle est bougonne;
La taupe, elle, n'y voit pas;
Le papillon ne hait personne. . . .

L'écho de ce pays est sûr.
J'observe, je suis bon prophète;
Je vois tout de mon petit mur,
Même tituber la chouette. . . .
                    [LM, 26–27]

———

Let the sunflower keep its seeds—
Your cypress trees would be distressed,
Goldfinch, spread your wings again,
Go back to your wooly nest. . . .

Man would shoot you down—watch out!
The sunflower is on his side;
Only the grass belongs to you,
The folding grass where you can hide.

The snake will not know who you are,
From grasshoppers talk is hard won;
As for moles, they cannot see;
Butterflies don't hate anyone. . . .

Trust the echo of this land.
From my low wall I spy on fate;
Nothing will escape my eye:
Sometimes the owl can't fly straight! . . .
Patricia Terry

Here, the lizard-poet guides the "léger gentil roi des cieux" ["airy gentle ruler of the skies"], the goldfinch, away from the solitary sunflower—which would act as a frame or spotlight, exposing the bird as nakedly as did the warbler's willow—and into the collective grasses, akin to reeds, peopled by a host of small, unhostile, fleeting creatures whose complicity will act as dual protection for the fugitive. One of Char's wartime entries, when it was he and not the goldfinch who needed shelter and support, invokes this same populace:

> Le peuple des prés m'enchante. Sa beauté frêle et dépourvue de venin, je ne me lasse pas de me la réciter. Le campagnol, la taupe, sombres enfants perdus dans la chimère de l'herbe, l'orvet, fils du verre, le grillon, moutonnier comme pas un, la sauterelle qui claque et compte son linge, le papillon qui simule l'ivresse et agace les fleurs de ses hoquets silencieux, les fourmis assagies par la grande étendue verte, et immédiatement au-dessus les météores hirondelles. . . Prairie, vous êtes le boîtier du jour. [FM, 132]

The people of the meadows enchant me. Their frail beauty, totally without venom—I never get tired of reciting it to myself. The field mouse, the mole, dark children lost in the chimera of the grass, the green snake, son of glass, the cricket more than a little sheep-like, the grasshopper who snaps and counts her linen, the butterfly who simulates drunkenness, annoying the flowers with his silent hiccups, the ants taught wisdom by the great green expanse, and, just above, the meteor swallows. . .
Meadow, you are day's container.

These delicate creatures are numerous, a gentle collective, minute and interlocking like the mechanism of a watch. Unlike men and unlike the nightmare of war, they are without venom. Both poet and goldfinch can take temporary refuge among them. But it is temporary for both, both live elsewhere. The goldfinch's true home, his woolen nest, is located in the cypress trees, which represent another cluster of security, in contrast to the solitary sunflower. And indeed, Char's invocation of the cypress as protective symbol is altogether natural, for in Provence the crops, like the poet's goldfinch and warbler, are not only sheltered from the wind by reed barriers, but these alternate with high dense walls of cypress trees.

Trees represent protection, then. However, they can also represent its opposite, exposure. They are the natural territory of the bird, a larder (they bear fruit), a nesting place, and airfield in the sky. But they are rooted in the earth, man's province—which makes matters more complex, and leads us into a consideration of the ambivalent and often apocalyptic interaction between birds, trees, and men in Char's poetic universe.

Both birds and trees are mirrors to the human creature: "L'oiseau et l'arbre sont conjoints en nous. L'un va et vient, l'autre maugrée et pousse" ["Bird and tree conjoin in us. One comes and goes, the other grows and grumbles"] (RBS, 163). In our rootedness, grumbling, tossed by the wind but stubbornly resilient, we resemble trees. That which takes wing in us, which sings and flies and shatters easily, is our bird portion. Elusive as the swift, whose pause is in the darkest hollow and whom no eyes can hold, that part of us flees into shadow, seeking shelter—which may be found, as we have seen, among the cypress or the reeds, or in the pleated meadow, but which is at its densest in "the partner forest" (NP, 60), the ultimate vegetable community. A friend to both men and birds, the longer the forest lasts, the deeper and taller and stronger it gets. "Dans nos jardins se préparent des forêts" ["In our gardens, forests prepare themselves"] (LPA, 154). We must give them time to grow:

POUR QU'UNE FORÊT. . .

Pour qu'une forêt soit superbe
Il lui faut l'âge et l'infini.
Ne mourez pas trop vite, amis

Du casse-croûte sous la grêle.
Sapins qui couchez dans nos lits
Eternisez nos pas sur l'herbe.

[CP, 161]

FOR A FOREST. . .

For a forest to be superb
It needs age and the infinite.
Do not die too quickly, friends
Of picnics under the hail.
Pines who sleep in our beds,
Perpetuate our footsteps on the grass.

This forest is potentially superb and yet familiar enough to share with us a picnic and a bed. We identify with it, and thus its potential age and stature send us back a glimmer of eternity. But the curious verse "Sapins qui couchez dans nos lits" indicates our shared mortality as well. Both firs and men are threatened, and when men die they lie quite literally with the spruce, itself dead, which forms their coffin. They are the closest of bedfellows, and resemble each other too in their manner of dying: both are felled by death, when they do not go straight up in flame. As Char describes a former comrade during the war, "Il portait ses quarante-cinq ans verticalement, tel un arbre de la liberté" ["He carried his forty-five years vertically, like a tree of liberty"] (FM, 128). In life, both trees and men stand upright.

"Debout" is a crucial word and posture for the poet (see "Louis Curel de la Sorgue" (FM, 41), "Fenaison" ["Hay Harvest"] (FM, 38), "Afin qu'il n'y soit rien changé" ["In Order that Nothing be Changed"] (FM, 31), "Le visage nuptial" ["The Nuptial Face"] (FM, 58), among other texts). "Comment agressés de toutes parts," writes the poet, "croqués, haïs, roués, arrivons-nous cependant à jouir, debout, debout, debout, avec notre exécration, avec nos reins?" ["How, provoked on all sides, snarled at, hated, beaten, how do we manage nonetheless to find pleasure, upright, upright, upright, with our execration, with our loins?"] (RBS, 169). We have already seen his chastised adolescent holding himself as straight and attentive as a reed. In "Pour qu'une forêt. . ." the great fir trees, while they stand, remind us of our own stature, seem to make our transience eternal. Our passing footsteps on the grass remain, imprinted, guarded over by the firs, our witness and our surrogate. And there are less majestic trees—the larch, the poplar—whom the poet claims as brothers too:

VERS L'ARBRE-FRÈRE AUX JOURS COMPTÉS

Harpe brève des mélèzes,
Sur l'éperon de mousse et de dalles en germe
—Façade des forêts où casse le nuage—,
Contrepoint du vide auquel je crois.

[LPA, 115]

TO FRIEND-TREE OF COUNTED DAYS

Brief harp of the larches
On mossy spur of stone crop
—Facade of the forest,
Against which mists are shattered—
Counterpoint of the void in which
    I believe.

William Carlos Williams

As brief as the brief harp of the larches (their days like the poet's and the warbler's are numbered, but they make music while they live) this poem is suspended in mid-air, mid-sentence. Char takes us up the mountain, clouds break like waves against the forest here. We are at life's uppermost, outermost limit, on a spur of moss and "dalles en germe": germinating stones, themselves fragmented, seedlike, at the top of the mountain—an image which recalls the poet's own night carvings on birch bark, half poem/half picture, in *La nuit talismanique* [*The Talismanic Night*], and his remark about how poems, in general, are written as though on scattered rocks...one here...one over there...another on that one..."[5] It recalls, too, the following image from a recent text: "La parole écrite s'installe dans l'avènement des jours comptés, sur une ardoise de hasard" ["The written word settles in the advent of counted days, on a chance slate..."] (CB, 30). Again, counted days and, in response, the written word—like the poems written on Pierre Reverdy's "ardoises du toit." This, in counterpoint to the void, to death, this fragile writing in which the poet puts his faith, this fragmentary ephemeral singing at the lip of the abyss.

It *is* ephemeral. Like birds and men, the brief harp of the larches, the poplar in "Effacement du peuplier" ["The Poplar Tree's

Effacement"] (NP, 15), even the splendid firs in "Pour qu'une forêt. . ." are threatened. Frost is their enemy (see "Lied du figuier" ["The Fig Tree's Lied"] [NP, 34]), as is the lightning, and, most ironically, man himself. For he is careless with matches ("Homme / J'ai peur du feu / Partout où tu te trouves" [MSM, 32] [Man / I am afraid of fire / Everywhere you are]); and he chops trees down:

> Le chêne et le gui se murmurent
> Les projets de leurs ennemis,
> Le bûcheron aux hanches dures,
> La faucille de l'enfant chétif.
> [LM, 16]

> The oak and the mistletoe murmur
> The plans of their enemies,
> The hard-boned woodsman,
> The blade of the puny child.

In Char's poetry, as in the world around him, man destroys even that with which he most strongly identifies. This unthinking reed, alone of all the poet's threatened creatures, does not seem to know what they know instinctively—that contact, proximity, any attempt at possession can destroy. Thus "les arbres ne se questionnent pas entre eux, mais trop rapprochés, ils font le geste de s'éviter" ["trees do not question each other; rather, when too close, they shy away. . ."] (NT, 62).[6] The friendship and deep analogy between men, trees, and birds lends even more poignancy to the poet's melancholy, possessive hunter, who shoots birds "pour que l'arbre lui reste" ["so that the tree will remain his"] (LM, 13) and with the same bullet sets the forest on fire.

CHAPTER 2
THE MELANCHOLY HUNTER

"Ce sont les pessimistes qui l'avenir élève. [LPA, 152]

"It is pessimists who are raised by the future.

ALL OF CHAR'S BIRDS AND BEASTS LIVE IN
the perpetual presence of danger, most usually personified by the
hunter's gun. But this threatening presence only serves to heighten
their beauty:

ÉBRIÉTÉ
Tandis que la moisson achevait de se graver sur le cuivre
du soleil, une alouette chantait dans la faille du grand vent sa
jeunesse qui allait prendre fin. L'aube d'automne parée de ses
miroirs déchirés de coups de feu, dans trois mois retentirait.
[AC, 31]

INEBRIATION
While the harvest finished etching itself on the sun's copper, a lark sang in a fault of the great wind its youth which
was to end. Autumn's dawn, bejeweled with mirrors torn by
gunshot, in three months would resound.

In this poem full of jagged mirrors and distorted images, what the
lark sings so ebulliently is her own ending. As in "Congé au vent,"
the wind has fallen for a moment, and the future harvest, not yet
fully grown, is in the process of engraving itself on the copper disk
of the sun. (One sees the pointed Charian crops, upright, fields full
of engraver's tools.) Three months from this still yellow instant, as
the wind is rising and the harvest being cut—its completed image
pulled from the plate of the sun—the lark will be cut down, seduced
by all the mirrors set out to attract her in the autumn dawn. Gunfire
will answer then to her inebriated song: two passionate enuncia-

THE MELANCHOLY HUNTER   21

tions, echoing. Her coming death, her inevitable coupling with the hunter's bullet gives to the present moment its intensity.

The hunter, then, is more than simply a destructive force. He helps to create the beauty of his prey, whose ephemerality matches his own. And because this is so, and because the two of them are caught up in a drama over which neither seems to exercise control, there exists a kind of passionate reciprocity between these "loyal adversaries," the two halves of the hunt. They fascinate each other. Thus far, we have considered the pursued and some of its defenses: invisibility, muteness, reliance on the complicity of other creatures and on the natural vegetation around it. Let us now look at the pursuer and his weapons.

He is, to begin with, invisible. He lies in wait for his prey, camouflaged, mute, and sly—just like the warbler who evades him. The swift is no slimmer than his gun, the snake scarcely quicker to disappear than he. Depending on what he is hunting, his weapons and techniques may differ, as well as his moral character, but his own invisibility remains essential to the kill. As in the opening of Char's play, *Le Soleil des eaux* [*The Sun of Waters*]:

Octobre 1946. Pointe de l'aube. Colline boisée. Chant de grives. Un coup de feu part. Chant de grives. Au pied d'un arbre, une cage couverte d'herbes. Dans le taillis, à quelques pas, un chasseur. Deux grives dans la cage chantent: ce sont des appelants. Autour de la cage, sur le sol, des oiseaux morts, un merle agonisant. Silhouette du chasseur à l'affût. Il se redresse. Il nous parle.

Le chasseur, à voix basse:

Je suis chasseur de mon métier et un peu paysan. Mon village, Saint-Laurent, est un vieux village; il existait déjà du temps des Croisades. Ses habitants étaient tous des pêcheurs. [TCA, 87]

———

October, 1946. First dawn. Hillside forest. Call of a thrush. A shot rings out. Call of a thrush. At the foot of a tree, a cage covered with grass. In the undergrowth, a few feet away, a hunter. Two thrushes in the cage are singing: they are decoys. Around the cage, on the ground, dead birds, a dying blackbird. Silhouette of the hunter lying in wait. He straightens up. He addresses us.

The hunter, in a low voice:

I'm a hunter by profession and something of a peasant. My village, Saint-Laurent, is an old village. It already existed at the time of the Crusades. Its inhabitants were all fishermen.

Dawn, 1946: a resonant hour, peopled only by the invisible hunter and his two caged thrushes who call to their death the birds around them. Immediately, the hunter establishes himself and his violent activity within the context of French history. Like Proust's Françoise, he is at least in part the immemorial French peasant, not so far removed from the Crusades. His is an old village, its traditional profession fishing. Thus, the hunt comes out of French tradition and perpetuates it, and the professional hunter is no villain. In fact, in this play he is a revolutionary figure, a celebrant of "le devoir forcé de la révolte, victorieuse ou défaite, jamais vaine" ["the necessary duty of revolt, victorious or defeated, never fruitless"] (TCA, 214). He is a hero. And this is frequently the case in Char's work—although there are some notable exceptions: the Nazis hunted the Maquis; there is nothing heroic about Nazis, nor about the crazy hunter Carafon in the play *Sur les hauteurs* [*On the Heights*]. He wantonly kills hares, is perceived as dangerous from the outset, "parce que derrière ton fusil, tu prends les bêtes pour des gens" ["because behind your gun, you mistake animals for people"] (TCA, 18), and ends by shooting to death the play's lovers.

Although they may be referred to as "hunters," Carafon and the Nazis are in fact murderers. It is the blurring of the difference between these two professions, the erasure of the line between the kind of violence practiced by the murderer and the kind of violence practiced by the passionate Charian hunter, which has been called by René Girard "the *sacrificial crisis*. . .loss of the difference between impure violence and purifying violence. When this difference is lost, there is no longer any purification possible, and impure violence, which is contagious—that is, reciprocal—spreads throughout the community."[1] This description fits the Occupation all too well. Hence Char's scrupulous surveillance of his own violence. He writes: "Les jours de pluie nettoie ton fusil. (Entretenir l'arme, la chose, le mot? Savoir distinguer la liberté du mensonge, le feu du feu criminel)" ["On rainy days clean your gun. (How to keep the weapon, the thing, the word, in good condition? Be able to distinguish between freedom and lies, fire and criminal fire.)"] (RBS, 164). What determines the difference between fire and criminal fire—the former associated with freedom, the latter with lies—is the dual identity of hunter and hunted; who is being shot, who is doing the shooting, and why. Nor is it simply a question of whether the prey is human or not. Sometimes it is necessary to kill human beings, as in the following passage from "Feuillets d'Hypnos":

> Olivier le Noir m'a demandé une bassine d'eau pour nettoyer son revolver. Je suggérai la graisse d'arme. Mais c'est bien l'eau qui convenait. Le sang sur les parois de la cuvette demeurait hors de portée de mon imagination. A quoi eût servi de se représenter la silhouette honteuse, effondrée, le canon dans l'oreille, dans son enroulement gluant? Un justicier rentrait, son labeur accompli, comme un qui, ayant bien rompu sa terre, décrotterait sa bêche avant de sourire à la flambée de sarments. [FM, 143]

> Olivier le Noir asked me for a pan of water to clean his revolver. I suggested gun oil. But he needed water all right. The blood on the sides of the basin was beyond the reach of my imagination. What good would it have done to picture the shameful silhouette, the gun at his ear, as he sank into a sticky writhing? An executor of justice was coming home, his work done, just as one who having broken his ground would clean off his spade before smiling at the fire of vineshoots.

Olivier le Noir is a just man who, like the farmer, does his job, takes good care of his tools, needs a wash before he settles down in front of the fire. But what a tragic difference between the two. Still, when one is a shepherd, Char says, one has to kill the wolf. Most Charian hunters do not commit crimes, and there is a strong identification between them and the poet throughout his work, an identification which is complicated and enriched by the fact that both identify equally with their prey. Thus, in *Le soleil des eaux* a community of trout fishermen is betrayed by a man who catches eels for a living. Slimy, solitary, treacherous. Fishermen and hunters wear the colors and adopt the character—if they did not already have it—of the particular creature they choose to go after.

Nowhere is this relationship between hunter and hunted more clearly expressed than in one of the "documents" attached to the text of the play. In a kind of appendix entitled "Pourquoi du *Soleil des eaux*: témoignages et documents" ["The Why of *The Sun of Waters*: Testimony and documents"], we find the following statement about the fishermen along the Sorgue, spoken by an exfisherman, Marius Dimier, in language resembling Char's in his simplest and most tender passages:

Il faut vivre avec le poisson. Vous parler des pêcheurs, c'est vous parler de disparus. J'étais le dernier. Je ne pêche plus.

De mon temps, la pêche était une profession qui groupait des dizaines de familles. . . .C'était un métier dur qui demandait beaucoup d'intelligence et de patience. Il faut vivre avec le poisson. . . .

Pour nous autres, c'était une vraie besogne. Il faut vivre avec le poisson. Nous avions des filets petits ou grands, l'aragnol ou l'épervier, et aussi des cordes de fond pour les anguilles. Mais une certaine réputation de sournoiserie s'est toujours attachée aux pêcheurs d'anguilles. La pêche la plus personnelle, c'était la pêche au trident qui demandait beaucoup de ruse, de coup d'oeil et d'adresse. Il faut vivre avec le poisson.

Hélas! tout cela est bien fini. . . .

On nous a chassés de notre rivière! Et les fils des derniers pêcheurs sont appelés des braconniers! Ils finissent toujours en prison, ne pouvant payer les amendes écrasantes qu'on leur inflige. . . .[Maintenant] j'exerce pour manger un métier d'idiot. Je ne suis pas heureux. Je ne vis plus avec le poisson.
[TCA, 216-218]

You have to live with the fish. To talk about the fishermen is to talk about people who've disappeared. I was the last. I don't fish anymore.

In my day, fishing as a profession grouped tens of families. . . .It was a difficult craft which required a lot of intelligence and patience. You have to live with the fish. . . .

For us, it was real work. You have to live with the fish. We had little nets and big nets, the *aragnol* and the *épervier*, and also bottom lines for the eels. But eel fishermen always had a certain reputation for underhandedness. The most personal kind of fishing was with the trident, which called for a lot of cunning, accuracy, and skill. You have to live with the fish.

Alas! All that's over. . . .

They chased us away from our river! And the sons of the last fishermen are called poachers! They always end up in jail, not being able to pay the crushing fines inflicted on them. . . [Now] in order to eat I do the job of an idiot. I'm not happy. I don't live with the fish anymore.

"Le chasseur est chassé," ["The hunter is hunted"], as Char has said.[2] Forces more powerful than he conspire against him, just as he conspires against his prey. Except that the fisherman loves his fish. This is the paradox of their relationship. He loves his fish and lives with them, yet his life depends on their death. And this is how it should be, this is in the order of things, in the natural world. What is unnatural is for fish to die of chemicals. Pollution is in no way "nuptial destruction," there is no passion in it, only sterile killing. And so in *Le soleil des eaux* it is the polluting of their river by industry that causes the community of fishermen to revolt. Economics is basic to their uprising, but just as fundamental and as fundamentally enraging is the fact that the industrialists are assaulting all of nature. And they are destroying an art form, as well.

For fishing is an art. And thus it acts on one level as a metaphor for the making of poetry and comes to radiate ambiguity and paradox. This is characteristically Charian. So too is the fact that the fishermen and their fish find themselves enacting a major drama, involved in a confrontation that raises ethical questions far larger than themselves. Char writes, of *Le soleil des eaux*: "Circonscrits, l'éternel mal, l'éternel bien y luttent sous les figures minimes de la truite et de l'anguille. Des pêcheurs portent leurs couleurs" ["Eternal good, eternal evil, circumscribed, struggle there in the minimal forms of trout and eel. Fishermen wear their colors."] (TCA, 83). This is a play about revolution, resistance to the forces of evil, economic repression, the death of the natural world. But here, the grand themes of brotherhood and betrayal are acted out by local peasants, and Good and Evil are symbolized by creatures no bigger than the warbler in the reeds.

There is essentially no big game in Char's poetic universe (the two possible exceptions to this rule being the bull and the eagle, neither of which participates in the hunt as we are looking at it now); there are only big themes. Cosmic struggles occur between a goldfinch and a hunter who goes home to lunch, while butterflies and lizards look on. We have already seen this combination of the familiar and the superb in "Pour qu'une forêt. . . ." It is fundamental to every nature poem Char has written. His prey is never royal, no stags or wild boar; eels replace white whales. Simple animals are killed, as simple as the men who kill them. Char's phrase "commune présence" takes on new meaning. The adjective refers not only to the collective aspect of the poet's world and to the shared identity of man, beast, and tree. It is also a class distinction. This poet is interested in the common man, the common bird—especially in those uncommon moments when they transcend themselves and, in a flash, are gone. It is the pressure of death that leads to such transcendence and the fact of death—the frequency of killing—that towers in Char's universe. And it is precisely this juxtaposition of the minimal and the infinite that moves us in his bird-and-beast poems. The unassuming warbler, having braved the eye of the gun, sings suddenly the deepest song. She is made to the measure of ordinary men, as insignificant as they, as fragile, and, like them, with the stunning power of beauty in her, what Martin Heidegger has called "the splendor of the simple."³ This may be said, too, of the elusive swift and the sparkling trout, and of the melancholy hunter.

Neither aristocrat nor foreigner (although he *is* a loner and, as such, in perpetual exile), the hunter seems to be as much a part of nature as his prey, whom, as we have seen, he profoundly resembles. Morally, he takes on the character of the animal he hunts. Strategically, he adopts the same ruses as his quarry: camouflage, invisibility, silence, stealth. In stature, he is not much bigger than his adversary, nor much longer lived, at least against the background of the cosmos. The hunter is as breakable, as evanescent, as easily fascinated by what destroys him as the lark, and like her he is doomed. *Le chasseur est chassé.*

He is doomed not simply because he is mortal, but also because he is a prey to the impossible and very human desire for permanence. He wishes to possess what cannot be possessed, to preserve a world as changing as himself. And the hunter's tragedy is compounded by the fact that his means of reaching out toward the world is his weapon. The gun is an extension of himself; it is through the gun that he transcends his solitude and steps out of his separateness toward union with the world around him. His bullet connects, communicates with his quarry, and destroys it. The hunter's union with the bird is an explosion. By reaching for it, he annihilates what he wishes to hold onto.

But this, if it is his tragedy (not to mention the goldfinch's), is also his transcendence, for it does away with *accumulation* and its negative equivalent, *decay*. Nothing is more deadening than these to the poet, who covets permanence as much as his hunter does but knows that holding onto things and people yields not permanence but slow corruption. As we said of "Congé au vent," relinquishment lies at the heart of the Charian experience.

Thus, in the love poem "Marthe" Char writes:

Je n'entrerai pas dans votre coeur pour limiter sa
mémoire. Je ne retiendrai pas votre bouche pour l'empêcher
de s'entr'ouvrir sur le bleu de l'air et la soif de partir. Je veux
être pour vous la liberté et le vent de la vie qui passe le seuil
de toujours avant que la nuit ne devienne introuvable. [FM, 191]

I will not enter your heart to limit its memory. I will not
take your mouth to hinder its opening on the blue of the air
and the thirst for departure. I want to be freedom for you,
and the wind of life which crosses the threshold of always
before night becomes undiscoverable.

All things corrode. Even roses are exquisite only for a day, then
fade, then putrify. And the same may be said of birds. Left alone,
they perish slowly of old age—and boredom, one suspects,—in
Char's universe. What was pure flight and song, quickness, color,
dazzling fragility, slows down, thickens, disappears, but without
grace. This is what the hunter saves his prey from when he destroys
it, this negative form of duration, synonymous with slow death, the
exact opposite of the brief, intense, lightning-like duration coveted
by the poet: "Si nous habitons un éclair, il est le coeur de l'éternel"
["If we dwell in a lightning bolt, it is the heart of the eternal"] (FM,
198).

The hunter, then, is a kind of unwitting, unwilling hero. It
makes him sad (*mélancolique* is Char's word). He loves trees and
birds, but cannot touch them—or even see them—without their going up in flames. Each time he leaves his house and enters the
natural world, that world ceases to be peaceful. His arrival signals
disaster, he is a disruptive force. Hence the poet's respect for him:
"Ce qui vient au monde pour ne rien troubler ne mérite ni égards ni
patience" ["That which comes into the world to cause no trouble
merits neither respect nor patience"] (FM, 195). The hunter is a true
rebel in that he practices "la vraie violence (qui est révolte)" ["true
violence (which is revolt)"] (RBS, 166), and practices it without
venom. He kills but remains a life force, not simply because he stirs
things up, but also because, like the poet, his explosive act is born of
desire. And when violence is coupled with love, it is "magique"
(LM, 43). It heralds:

. . .la venue d'une réalité qui sera sans concurrente. Imputrescible celle-là. Impérissable, non; car elle court les dangers de tous. Mais la seule qui visiblement triomphe de la mort matérielle. Telle est la Beauté, la Beauté hauturière, apparue dès les premiers temps de notre coeur, tantôt dérisoirement conscient, tantôt lumineusement averti. [LPA, 197]

. . .the coming of a peerless reality. Incorruptible. Not imperishable, for it runs the same dangers as everyone. But the only reality that visibly triumphs over material death. Such is Beauty, the Beauty of the high seas, present ever since our hearts' earliest days, hearts sometimes absurdly conscious, sometimes luminously aware.

It is precisely this kind of beauty that the hunter's bullet creates in Char's long, half-sung poem, "Fête des arbres et du chasseur" ["Celebration of the Trees and the Hunter"], for when his bullet sets the forest on fire, what goes up in flame is the perishable part. Leaves lose their substance to light, earth becomes air. What remains—fire, poetry—is incorruptible, as poets know, or dream: "Seuls aux fenêtres des fleuves / Les grands visages éclairés / Rêvent qu'il n'y a rien de périssable / Dans leur paysage carnassier" ["Alone at the windows of rivers / The great enlightened faces / Dream there is nothing perishable / In their carnivorous landscape"] (MSM, 76). The bullet pulverizes and illuminates like its equivalent in the natural world, lightning—which also causes forest fires—or its equivalent in the world of poetry, the metaphor. The hunter's fiery gesture makes him an artist:

Les deux guitares exaltent dans la personne du chasseur mélancolique (il tue les oiseaux "pour que l'arbre lui reste" cependant que sa cartouche met du même coup le feu à la forêt) l'exécutant d'une contradiction conforme à l'exigence de la création. [LM, 13]

The two guitars exalt in the person of the melancholy hunter (he kills birds "so the tree will remain his" and with his smoking cartridge sets the forest on fire), one who acts out a contradiction consistent with the exigencies of creation.

He lights up the sky and preserves the forest for us as it was, in our memory: "Forêt qui subsistez dans l'émotion de tous. . . / Devant l'étincelle du vide, / Vous n'êtes jamais seule, ô grande disparue!" ["Forest still alive in the hearts of everyone. . . / Before the spark of the void, / You are never alone, who have disappeared!"] (LM, 20). The forest is gone but continues to live, henceforth invisible, except in our mind's eye. And there we also carry a second image: of the forest transformed into fire, all its disparate elements newly merged in "l'étendue embrasée des forêts. . .maintenant livrée à la solidarité de l'éclatement et de la destruction" ["the blazing expanse of forests. . .now given over to the solidarity of explosion and destruction"] (LPA, 125). Char's hunter has defeated death over time. He participates in the sacred—"Violence and the sacred are inseparable"[4]—for he practices a purifying violence. He is a poet. Like Char, his is a "métier de pointe" ["a pointed métier"] (LPA, 147): both the pen and the arrow are pointed, both the bullet and the poet's words are piercing. Like the poet, the hunter takes aim—he *sights*, the poet *sees*. Like the poet, the hunter fires—and the illuminative synthesis of bullet and tree is equivalent to the poetic image, in which opposites collide and give off light as they are metamorphosed:

> Pourquoi *poème pulvérisé* ? Parce qu'au terme de son voyage vers le Pays, après l'obscurité pré-natale et la dureté terrestre, la finitude du poème est lumière, apport de l'être à la vie. [LPA, 147. Char's italics]

> Why *pulverized poem*? Because at the end of its journey Home, after prenatal darkness and the hardness of the earth, the finitude of the poem is light, being's contribution to life.

CHAPTER 3
VENERY

*Ici l'image mâle poursuit sans se lasser
l'image femelle, ou inversement.
Quand elles réussissent à s'atteindre,
c'est là-bas la mort du créateur et
la naissance du poète.* [MSM, 134]

*Here the male image tirelessly pursues
the female image, or inversely.
When they succeed in overtaking
each other—there, the creator dies and
the poet is born.*

THE READER CANNOT HELP BUT BE STRUCK BY
the ferocity—or, to use Char's own term, the "fureur"—with which
the poet conceives of his own profession. To write is to commit an
act of violence, albeit nuptial, purifying violence. Char's is a
universe where, as we have noted, silence accompanies wholeness
and words break things, where the poet is a seer and seeing is
equated with pulling the trigger. The act of creation is filled with
turbulence. Not only for the poet as he works, but also for his
reader. Poetry is explosive. It is also subversive:

> Arthur Rimbaud jaillit en 1871 d'un monde en agonie, qui
> ignore son agonie et se mystifie, car il s'obstine à parer son
> crépuscule des teintes de l'aube de l'âge d'or. . . .
> L'enfant de Charleville se dirige à pied vers Paris. Con-
> temporain de la Commune, et avec d'analogues représailles, il
> troue de part en part comme une balle l'horizon de la poésie
> et de la sensibilité. Il voit, relate et disparaît. . . .[RBS, 122–123]

> Arthur Rimbaud flashes forth in 1871 from a dying world,
> unaware of its dying, which fools itself by stubbornly adorn-
> ing its own twilight with the tints of dawn of the golden
> age. . . .
> Charleville's child makes his way on foot to Paris. A con-
> temporary of the Commune, and with analogous reprisals,
> bullet-like, he punctures the horizon of poetry and emotion
> through and through. He sees, tells, and disappears. . . .

The effect of Rimbaud's vision-narration-disappearance is
equivalent to the effect of the Commune. (Still another resonance in

"Commune présence.") The seer-poet is a revolutionary gunman. With his eyes and words—with his *voyance*—he shoots holes in the horizon. Not only does this change the way other men see; it also satisfies their hunger for violence: "Les hommes ont faim / De viandes secrètes, d'outils cruels," writes Char. "Levez-vous, bêtes à égorger, / A gagner le soleil" ["Men are hungry / For secret meat, cruel implements. / Rise up, beasts for the slaughtering, / To win the sun"] (MSM, 21).

We have already seen that the poet identifies with his hunters—and with their prey as well. And if poetry, like hunting, is capable of assuaging man's craving for secret meat and cruel implements, this is because poetry is itself mysterious nourishment and at the same time a piercing tool. It contains within it both the sacrificial animal and the weapon; it is the explosive sum of the two. Jean-Pierre Richard has compared it to a bullfight: "All poetry is. . .in some sense bullfighting: mutual, ritual murder of certain objects or concepts brought together by force, in order that like the dying bull they may give off a kind of black light. The resultant obscurity of the poem is doubtless nothing other than the dazzlement springing from an execution of the impossible, from antithesis transformed into identity."[1]

If we pursue this analogy, we must identify the "poète carnassier" ["the carnivorous poet"] (MSM, 79) as both bull and matador. He is "le chasseur de soi" ["the self-hunter"] (FM, 171), his poem the sum of his own contradictions as they meet each other head on: "Au centre de la poésie, un contradicteur t'attend. C'est ton souverain. Lutte loyalement contre lui" ["At the center of poetry a contradictor awaits you. He is your sovereign. Fight him loyally"] (RBS, 165). In each of his poems, as he wields the weapon, his eyes, his words, Char is the hunter. As he risks himself—that self is, in part, what he and we are looking for—he is the prey, slipping into sight for the length of a heartbeat, like the young viper: "Il glisse contre la mousse du caillou comme le jour cligne à travers le volet" ["He slides past the pebble's moss the way the day winks through the shutter"] (LPA, 129); like the warbler: "La perche de saule happée est à l'instant cédée par l'ongle de la fugitive" ["Her fugitive claw grapples and gives up at once a perch in the willow"]; like the swift: "L'été de la longue clarté, il filera dans les ténèbres, par les persiennes de minuit" ["In the long brilliance of summer, he slips through the shutters of midnight into shadow"] (FM, 214); then fleeing back, or pretending to flee, like the snake: "Par le lien qui unit la lumière à la peur, / Tu fais semblant de fuir, ô serpent marginal" ["Along the line uniting light and fear, / O marginal snake! you seem to run away"] (LPA, 108) into invisibility. Poetry is venery—with the poet playing all the roles—of which bullfighting may be said to be one variant.

But as Jean-Pierre Richard points out, the bullfight is highly ritualized, there is little improvisation involved and no chance of escape for the animal, even if he kills his opponent. Bullfighting represents the enforced confrontation of opposites (Richard's definition of the poetry of René Char). There is little place in a bullfight for *chance*, and this is not true of the hunt. The bull is trapped, encircled. But the birds and snakes and fish in Char's hunt poems all have a measure of freedom: the lark, for instance, "Carillon maître de son haleine et libre de sa route" ["Carillon, master of breathing and free to go where she will"] (LPA, 109). Chance blows around these free creatures like the wind, and they escape, if barely. They retain their freedom as long as they can avoid being seen (i.e., shot). Small wonder that "les oiseaux libres ne souffrent pas qu'on les regarde" ["free birds refuse to be looked at"] (LPA, 154). They are characterized not by a thundering charge forward, but a lightning takeoff in the opposite direction. Like Char's poetry, they are the embodiment of elusiveness:

LE MARTINET

Martinet aux ailes trop larges, qui vire et crie sa joie autour de la maison. Tel est le coeur.

Il dessèche le tonnerre. Il sème dans le ciel serein. S'il touche au sol, il se déchire.

Sa repartie est l'hirondelle. Il déteste la familière. Que vaut dentelle de la tour?

Sa pause est au creux le plus sombre. Nul n'est plus à l'étroit que lui.

L'été de la longue clarté, il filera dans les ténèbres, par les persiennes de minuit.

Il n'est pas d'yeux pour le tenir. Il crie, c'est toute sa présence. Un mince fusil va l'abattre. Tel est le coeur.

[FM, 214]

THE SWIFT

Swift whose wings are too wide, who spirals and cries out his joy around the house. The heart is like that.

He dries up the thunder. He sows in the quiet sky. If he touches the ground, he breaks.

The swallow is his counterpart. He detests her domesticity. What good is the tower's lace?

He will pause in the darkest crevice. None is more stringently lodged than he.

In the long brilliance of summer, he slips through the shutters of midnight into shadow.

No eyes can hold him. His presence is all in his cry. A slender gun is going to strike him down. The heart is like that.

Patricia Terry

The swift resembles the warbler in his invisibility, although it is his speed and not his settling into the community of reeds that makes him so.[2] He rivals the lightning—who but these two could dry up the thunder? He has nothing but contempt for the domesticated swallow, who flies round and round the tower while he himself goes shooting through the shades of midnight ("Certains se confient à une imagination toute ronde. Aller me suffit." ["Some put their trust in a round imagination. Straight ahead will do for me."] [FM, 22]). A slim gun is going to bring him down. But not yet, not while he remains invisible. He is as much the essence of Char's poetry as is the bullfight. He is ellipsis imaged. What Richard's bullfight analogy does not account for is precisely this: how much of Char's work is ellipsis, how evasive is his prey. His art is an attempt to capture that which eludes him (the swift), that which disappears the instant that he touches it (the burning forest). He writes, "Le poète ne retient pas ce qu'il découvre; l'ayant transcrit, le perd bientôt. En cela réside sa nouveauté, son infini et son péril" ["The poet does not hold onto what he discovers; having transcribed it, soon loses it. This makes him new, infinite, endangered"] (LPA, 147). Often, what Char transcribes is the very elusiveness of the things he is trying to discover, to see and tell. This is true in "La truite," in "Le martinet," and in the following brief but central text:

PERMANENT INVISIBLE

Permanent invisible aux chasses convoitées,
Proche, proche invisible et si proche à`mes doigts,
O mon distant gibier la nuit où je m'abaisse
Pour un novice corps à corps.
Boire frileusement, être brutal répare.
Sur ce double jardin s'arrondit ton couvercle.
Tu as la densité de la rose qui se fera.

[NP, 79]

PERMANENT INVISIBLE

Permanent invisible of coveted hunting grounds,
Close, close, invisible and almost in my hands,
O my distant quarry, those nights when I sink down
To novice flesh against flesh.
Drinking against the cold, being brutal restores.
Over this double garden you form a rounded dome
You are solid as the rose which is to be.
Patricia Terry

The prey in this poem is elusiveness itself. No longer even symbolized by the swift or the snake, what the poet hunts here is permanent invisibility in the flesh. He is out to capture that which is, by definition, absolutely and for all time beyond his reach, and which, paradoxically, the poem captures. For the poem embodies it—embodies something, that is, which has no body, no density at all, no more density than "la rose qui se fera." This is remarkable poetic alchemy: transforming something never seen but always there into a definite image, the rose, but the rose before it exists.

That which has been implicit elsewhere (in "La fauvette des roseaux," for example) becomes explicit here: permanence and invisibility are inseparable. What cannot be seen lasts, what lasts cannot be seen; the visible perishes. Explicit, too, for the first time is the connection between hunting, poetry, and love-making. The first and last of these activities have been associated with each other since time immemorial; they are both venery. And so, as we have seen, is Char's poetry. All are structurally similar, all are violent but constructive. In "Permanent invisible" it is the contact with his lover—"brutal" contact, let us note—that enables the poet to approach his distant game. Through this most physical of acts, this "novice corps à corps" with a being as impermanent and visible as he, he almost touches the least physical, most elusive, and therefore most enduring of realities. But ultimately it is the poem, not the woman, that captures that reality.

————

The connection here established between hunting, poetry, and eroticism leads us to consider the deeply sexualized nature of Char's poetic universe and, most particularly, of his bestiary. Maurice Blanchot has suggested in *L'Entretien infini* that one of the sources of Char's greatness is what Blanchot calls his "pensée du neutre." The critic isolates certain terms in the poet's vocabulary that are, in effect, grammatically neuter such as "l'inconnu" (the unknown) as it appears in the Charian question-affirmation: "*Comment vivre sans inconnu devant soi?*" [*"How can we live without the unknown ahead of us?"*].[3] Certainly the permanent invisible would find its place among these genderless terms. But if for Blanchot it is Char's ability to welcome the neutral infinite unknown into his poetry that makes him great, for this reader it is the finite, ephemeral, sexualized aspect of Char's poetic universe that gives to his work its deepest resonance.[4] His is the dialectic of desire, and in his poetry natural forces and phenomena, lightning, rivers, plants, even inanimate objects (e.g., windowpanes) are sexualized, deeply influenced by their dictionary-given gender—none more so than the creatures in the hunter-hunted poems we have been considering.

If we look again, for instance, at "le martinet" and "la fauvette des roseaux," we see that Char is equally tender toward both, but that his choice of imagery and the kind of behavior he ascribes to each differs profoundly. Whereas she (the warbler) settles down in a cluster of reeds to sing a sustained and all-encompassing song, he (the swift) is all sharpness and speed. And within his own poem, "Sa repartie est l'hirondelle. Il déteste la familière. Que vaut dentelle de la tour?" Feminine creatures tend to seek shelter, or at least to settle, more readily than their male counterparts (except for Char's captivated lizard who spends a great deal of time in his stone nest, observing). Thus, in "Ni éternel ni temporel," ["Neither Eternal nor Temporal"] the poet speaks of "l'alouette, l'oiseau qui se pose, le corbeau, l'esprit qui se grave" ["the lark, the bird who alights, the crow, the mind engraving itself"] (NP, 83). As might be expected, male creatures act in sharper, more aggressive—phallic—ways. One thinks immediately of the masculine oriole whose song, a sword, closes the sad bed (FM, 33) and of Char's two-pointed sun, the bull.

This brings us to "Quatre fascinants," a wonderful poem about birds, beasts, and the hunt, in which grammatical gender plays a crucial role, a text, too, which makes it clear that *seeing* and *being seen* are inextricably bound up with the Charian dialectic of desire. Blanchot comments quite accurately that the neutral unknown does not exist in the dimension of the visible/invisible, but in another dimension altogether. However, all the poems we have been considering take place precisely in the dimension of the visible/invisible—this is the space that mortal men and warblers inhabit—and they take their tension from the fact that here to be seen is to perish.

QUATRE FASCINANTS

Le taureau

Il ne fait jamais nuit quand tu meurs,
Cerné de ténèbres qui crient,
Soleil aux deux pointes semblables.

Fauve d'amour, vérité dans l'épée
Couple qui se poignarde unique parmi tous.

La truite

Rives qui croulez en parure
Afin d'emplir tout le miroir,
Gravier où balbutie la barque
Que le courant presse et retrousse,
Herbe, herbe toujours étirée,
Herbe, herbe jamais en répit,
Que devient votre créature
Dans les orages transparents
Où son coeur la précipita?

Le serpent

Prince des contresens, exerce mon amour
A tourner son Seigneur que je hais de n'avoir
Que trouble répression ou fastueux espoir.

Revanche à tes couleurs, débonnaire serpent,
Sous le couvert du bois et en toute maison.
Par le lien qui unit la lumière à la peur,
Tu fais semblant de fuir, ô serpent marginal!

L'alouette

Extrême braise du ciel et première ardeur du jour,
Elle reste sertie dans l'aurore et chante la terre agitée,
Carillon maître de son haleine et libre de sa route.

Fascinante, on la tue en l'émerveillant.

[LPA, 106–109]

FOUR WHO FASCINATE

The Bull

It is never dark when you die,
Rimmed with shouting shadows,
Twin-pointed sun.

Beast of love, the truth in a sword,
Crossed plunging blades: a unique couple.

The Trout

Crumbling rivershores, necklace
To fill up the whole mirror,
Pebbles below the babbling boat
Currents pull back and propel,
Grasses, grasses endlessly stretched out,
Grasses, grasses never left to rest,
What has become of your quick one
Among the transparent storms
Into which her heart swept her?

The Snake

Prince of twisted meanings, teach my love
To get around her Lord I hate whose scope
Is turbid repression, opulence of hope.

Now may your colors triumph, courtly snake,
Sheltered by the woods and in each house.
Along the line uniting light and fear,
O marginal snake! you pretend to run away.

The Lark

The sky's most extreme ember and first warmth of day,
Set into dawn she sings the unquiet earth,
Carillon, master of breathing and free to go where she will.

She fascinates, to be killed she must be dazzled.

Patricia Terry

Since these four creatures are so often read separately from one another,[5] it is worth reiterating that "Quatre fascinants" is one text, structurally and thematically unified. It progresses *upward*, from the heaviest, most earthbound animal, the bull, who is trapped by encircling shadows, yet at the same time portrayed as a sun, a burning sphere of energy ("Fire lives the death of earth," wrote Heraclitus)—through the feminine trout and the masculine snake: water and earth creatures—to the feminine lark, who sings and flies. She is the lightest of them all, the tiniest, she is *la Minutieuse* ["the Meticulous One"][6] and, for an instant, suspended in her element, the air, she is free. But the text is also *circular*, for the bull's verses are filled with light, total illumination, and he dies; and the same may be said of the lark ("and aer lives the death of fire," Heraclitus wrote[7]). The lark's verses too are full of light, she is the day's most intense ember, she glows, she too is on fire, and the evocation of her dying ends the poem. He dies (perpetually) in its first line; she is killed (perpetually) in its last. And each of these deaths is inevitable, for each creature is not only spotlighted but also encircled, the bull by shadows that cry out, the lark by the dawn in which she is "sertie": he is ringed in darkness, she in light. (This association of the male with darkness and the female with light immediately calls to mind Char's human lovers in poems such as "La chambre dans l'espace" ["The Room in Space"] (LPA, 138): "Je suis dans la grâce de ton visage que mes ténèbres couvrent de joie" ["I am in the grace of your countenance, which my shadows cover with joy"]. A verse immediately followed by a cry—"Comme il est beau ton cri qui me donne ton silence!" ["How beautiful your cry which gives me your silence!"]—a cry recalling the bull's "ténèbres qui crient" and the ecstatic song of the lark. Words, we have noted, break things. Sometimes what is broken out of, or into, is solitude. The lover's cry is a sign of union.) Between the bull and the lark, two fascinating creatures who are surrounded, illuminated and therefore vulnerable, Char places the trout and the snake, neither of whom dies in the poem (although both are threatened, as is every living creature in his poetry), neither of whom can be seen.

But if the two creatures who emerge into the light perish, there is a difference in their dying. "Le taureau" is as pointed as the masculine swift and the masculine crow, and he comes forward to knife his partner in the moment of his death. The lark, on the other hand, stops where she can be seen, a jewel; and when she goes forward to her death, it will be in a state of wonder, of "ébriété," hypnotized, fascinated. The bull and the matador are two violent, Charian adversary-lovers, "deux étrangers acharnés à se contredire—et à se fondre ensemble si leur rencontre aboutissait!" ["two strangers eager to contradict each other—and to merge, should their meeting succeed!"] (NP, 91–92). Which it does. But the lark will not knife anyone. What she will do is to fascinate her adversary. This is the reciprocity in her dying, this reciprocal bedazzlement, born of her beauty and of her lovely capacity for being astonished. The lark, like Eve, is seduced and a seductress; and her death, like that of the bull, must be read, at least on one level, as erotic.

As for the trout, she does not settle. Far from it, her whole poem is a landscape in movement, full of moving grasses (grass represents protection in Char's poetry, protection which she has relinquished) and glimmering water. Her heart propels her upward into transparent storms, into the foaming turbulence of waterfalls—this last, an image closely associated for the poet with love: in "Les premiers instants" ["The First Instants"], for example, the lovers are "poncés jusqu'à l'invisible" ["pumiced to invisibility"] by their waterfall (FM, 213). As is the trout. She goes forward, like the lark, in wonder. But we do not see her there. "Les orages transparents" and she exist outside the frame of the poem. She's gone. "Que devient votre créature. . . ?" asks the poet of those fixed, though constantly moving objects that she has abandoned, "rives, gravier, herbe. . ." "The trout has been united with the element that nourishes and enshrines [her]."[8] She eludes us, just like the snake.

But with the snake we once again come upon a difference in behavior that is connected to gender. "La truite" throws herself into her passions but, in her poem, takes no one along. "Le serpent" is actively subversive—at the poet's request (note that Char speaks directly to the masculine snake, as he does to the masculine bull, calling both "tu," while his feminine creatures remain a more distant "elle"):

Prince des contresens, exerce mon amour
A tourner son Seigneur que je hais de n'avoir
Que trouble répression ou fastueux espoir.

These first three lines of "Le serpent" are a fine example of Charian ellipsis as it shades into obscurity, and the poet's interpretation of them—which differs from that of most of his critics, but is borne out amply by the text itself—helps to illuminate them.[9] There is general agreement that his formal model is the medieval ballad, and that he invokes the snake as the medieval poet invoked his particular prince and protector. But "mon amour" is then habitually interpreted to refer to the poet's own emotion and the "Seigneur" in question is seen as God the Father. Now it seems to me that such a reading is only possible if "le serpent" is taken out of context. If we put him back where he belongs, namely, in the middle of "Quatre

fascinants," a text whose eroticism we have already seen in relation
to the pointed bull, the passionate trout, and the burning lark; if we
recall that most medieval ballads took as their subject courtly love,
"a code of chivalrous devotion to a married lady," and add to this
what we know from a reading of Char's other poetry—that he frequently addresses the woman with whom he is in love as "mon
amour," then these first three lines come clear.

The poet is asking the snake, that most classic of phallic sym-
bols, Eve's old friend and tutor, to teach the woman he loves the art
of evasion: Train her, Char urges, to get around her Lord (read: not
simply domineering husband, but all of society as it inhibits her, her
life force, her sensuality) whom I hate for being, by turns,
repressive, then ostentatiously tender. "Revanche à tes couleurs,
débonnaire serpent. . . !" The snake has been odd man out too long,
it is time for his colors—worn by the poet, of course—to triumph.

This marginal, phallic outlaw, the snake, is necessarily at the
center of "Quatre fascinants" (even if we cannot see him) for he
represents the imagination which must accompany desire—for the
forbidden—if that desire is to be realized; and he lives in
everybody's house and everybody's woods: "Sous le couvert du bois
et en toute maison." He is an intellectual, but in the service of
lubricity. He tempts, he disrupts the human world just as the hunter
disrupts the natural world, and he teaches us subversion,
evasiveness, camouflage. Pick up a log and there he is for an instant,
visible, frightening (men are afraid of snakes, and with reason) and
frightened (men kill snakes). In the instant of exposure, "par le lien
qui unit la lumière à la peur"—visibility is linked to death in Char's
poetic universe—he seems to flee, but doesn't. He disappears, but
remains close by. Elusive and ubiquitous, he is one form of the permanent invisible, perpetually in exile, "car, n'étant d'aucune
paroisse, il est meurtrier devant toutes" ["for, belonging to no
parish, he is a murderer to all"], and yet always there, flickering into
sight "comme le jour cligne à travers la volet" ["the way the day
winks through the shutter"] (LPA, 129), just when we were most
comfortable, to shake us up, to give us back our hunger, our
rebellion, our anguish. We need him, in his complexity. So the poet
sends the following telegram: "Réclamons venue civilisation
serpentaire. Très urgent" ["Demand advent serpentary civilization.
Extremely urgent"] (RBS, 168).

That the poet himself identifies with the snake must be obvious.
Like the hunter, they are both disquieted, disquieting creatures;
both take their power from their marginality; both practice "un

métier de pointe." Char writes elsewhere, "Le devoir d'un Prince est, durant la trêve des saisons et la sieste des heureux, de produire un Art à l'aide des nuages, un Art qui soit issu de la douleur et conduise à la douleur" ["A Prince's duty, during the truce of the seasons and the siesta of the contented, is to produce an Art with the help of the clouds, an Art which is born of pain and leads to pain"] (RBS, 161). Both the poet and his "Prince des contresens" inhabit pain and make their art from it. But Char's identification with the other creatures in "Quatre fascinants" is no less strong, and this is so whether they be male or female, bull, trout, or lark. They are all, like the poet, and like his warbler, his swift, sensual, threatened, luminous beings who live out, in the course of their poem, Char's admonition: "Emerge autant que possible à ta propre surface. Que le risque soit ta clarté" ["Rise to your own surface as much as possible. May risk be your brightness"] (RBS, 168). All four fascinating creatures go toward their risk, toward nuptial destruction, and it illuminates them like the rising sun in "Rougeur des Matinaux" ["Redness of the Matinals"]: the bull as he rushes to his piercing love-death, the trout flung forward into turbulence, the snake who slips through like the lightning, and the lark, ablaze, set into dawn and singing the agitated earth, oblivious (but not for long) to the mirrors torn by gunshot which surround her, fascinating, fascinated, in the moment of her death astonished.

Looking through his hunter's eyes, Char writes: "Nous sommes des météores à gueule de planète. Notre ciel est une veille, notre course une chasse, et notre gibier est une goutte de clarté" ["We are planet-faced meteors. Our sky is a vigil, our journey a hunt, and our prey a drop of light"] (RBS, 173). The bull, the trout, the snake, and the lark are all drops of light, caught by the poet with his own luminous words. Their poem is a series of illuminations, each of which unites light with fear: for the instant of visibility is the instant of death, even as it is the instant of creation. The poet is himself simultaneously lover, hunter, and creator of these poetic beasts. Poetry is his bullet and his hidingplace. Like the fisherman's trident, it pierces; like the fisherman's net, it is almost invisible as it encloses its prey. But that prey continues to live on the page, where the poem preserves its essence, which is elusiveness.

CHAPTER 4
LIGHTNING

*Si nous habitons un éclair, il
est le coeur de l'éternel.* [FM, 198]

*If we dwell in a lightning bolt,
it is the heart of the eternal.*

THE CELESTIAL EQUIVALENT OF CHAR'S MELAN-
choly hunter is the lightning. A swift, fatal, dazzling *trait d'union* between man and the cosmos, it illuminates and it destroys: "Nous
sommes ingouvernables. Le seul maître qui nous soit propice, c'est
l'Éclair, qui tantôt nous illumine et tantôt nous pourfend" ["We are
ungovernable. Our only propitious master is the Lightning, which
sometimes illuminates, sometimes splits us in two"] (LPA, 152). And
again:

> Mourir, ce n'est jamais que contraindre sa conscience, au
> moment même où elle s' abolit, à prendre congé de quelques
> quartiers physiques actifs ou somnolents d'un corps qui nous
> fut passablement étranger puisque sa connaissance ne nous
> vint qu'au travers d'expédients mesquins et sporadiques. Gros
> bourg sans grâce au brouhaha duquel s'employaient des
> habitants modérés. . .Et au-dessus de cet atroce hermétisme
> s'élançait une colonne d'ombre à face voûtée, endolorie et à
> demi aveugle, de loin en loin—ô bonheur—scalpée par la
> foudre. [FM, 72]
>
> ———
>
> Dying is never more than forcing one's consciousness, in
> the very moment it is abolished, to take leave of a few active
> or somnolent physical portions of a body that was fairly
> foreign to us, since our knowledge of it came only through
> makeshift means. A great graceless town whose hubbub
> engaged its moderate inhabitants. . .And above this atrocious
> hermeticism soared a column of shadow, its broken, tender,
> half-blind face now and again—o wonder!—scalped by light-
> ning.

We are strangers to ourselves, to the "atrocious hermeticism" of our own bodies, trapped in them while we live, separated from them when we die. The only moments of happiness are those in which our consciousness, a half-blind column of shadow—unseeing, unseeable—is scalped by a lightning bolt.

Lightning sometimes simply splits the sky, but often it streaks home, earthbound. Gathering itself in the celestial sphere, it shoots the earth, it hurtles down to set the earth on fire. For Char, lightning is as ubiquitous a threat, as essential a presence to men (and trees, their sometime surrogate) as is the hunter to the lark. It teaches us how to live: "Il n'y a plus de peuple-trésor, mais, de proche en proche, le savoir vivre infini de l'éclair pour les survivants de ce peuple" ["There is no longer a golden people, but increasingly the infinite *savoir vivre* of the lightning for the survivors of that people"] (NP, 91). It electrifies, enlightens, and sets us on fire, connecting not simply the cosmic and the terrestrial, but life and death themselves:

EFFACEMENT DU PEUPLIER

L'ouragan dégarnit les bois.
J'endors, moi, la foudre aux yeux tendres.
Laissez le grand vent où je tremble
S'unir à la terre où je crois.

Son souffle affile ma vigie.
Qu'il est trouble le creux du leurre
De la source aux couches salies!

Une clé sera ma demeure,
Feinte d'un feu que le coeur certifie;
Et l'air qui la tint dans ses serres.

[NP, 15]

THE POPLAR TREE'S EFFACEMENT

The hurricane is stripping the woods.
I lull the tender-eyed lightning to sleep.
Let the great wind where I tremble
Marry the earth where I grow.

Its breath sharpens my vigil.
How turbid it is, the hollow
Of the sullied streambed's lure!

A key will be my dwelling,
The feint of a fire the heart confirms;
And the air whose talon holds it.

We have already witnessed one forest fire, set by the melancholy hunter in "Fête des arbres et du chasseur." Therein, the trees were mute, they simply burned while the guitarists played and sang the praises of Char's inadvertent hero, the hunter. But here, in "Effacement du peuplier," we are being talked to by a poplar tree (in octosyllabic, rhymed verse), a rooted *fascinant*, whose brotherhood with men and martlets is obvious. The fragile poplar cannot move—until the lightning strikes, an explosive liberation—but it can stand up straight and lucid in the midst of storm, a "living pillar" given voice by Char, quite ready to be scalped by the tender-eyed lightning, which it cradles like a woman or a child.

Earth, air, fire, and water are all present in this poem, as they were in "Quatre fascinants," but it is air and fire that will triumph, as the poplar disappears, aflame, or remains standing, perhaps, but split in two: "déchiré." Already its perceptions are refined, its vigil sharpened ("mon métier est un métier de pointe") by the risen wind. As Char writes elsewhere, "La perception du fatal, la présence continue du risque. . .tiennent l'heure en haleine et nous maintiennent disponibles à sa hauteur" ["An awareness of the inevitable, the continual presence of risk. . .keep time suspended and us available at its height"] (RBS, 117). The poplar's heightened vision, heightened both literally and figuratively, separates it from the earth. Storm-tossed, it surveys the terrain around it, and sees "Qu'il est trouble le creux du leurre / De la source aux couches salies!" Turbulent waters: their lure that they irrigate the roots of the living tree and extinguish flame—but they are obscure and earthbound, muddied, whereas the poplar itself will shortly be all light, all fire, rising:

Une clé sera ma demeure,
Feinte d'un feu que le coeur certifie;
Et l'air qui la tint dans ses serres.

The key in which the poplar will reside (but keys open doors, they liberate—how can they be dwelt in?) is the lightning bolt which strikes it, carried in the talons of the air and fabricated of a fire that the heart and the air itself authenticate. This key-house requires authentication, for it is "feinte," that is, in some sense an artifice, a deception: the dwelling place, the liberation offered the tree are, in fact, death. But a fiery, spacious death, the kind Char covets—"La foudre spacieuse et le feu du baiser / Charmeront mon tombeau par l'orage dressé" ["The spacious lightning and the fire of a kiss / Will charm my tomb set up by the storm"] (LPA, 157)—a freeing from the earth by lightning, whose deepest witness is the heart, so that the poplar's essence (like the bull's, the lark's) is all that is left, its flesh transmuted into fire.

Or into poetry. As Jean Starobinski has suggested, the key in "Effacement du peuplier" is also the poem.[1] We said at the beginning of this essay that on the page it is the poet's disappearance that illuminates. In this, he resembles his meteor, his trout—and his poplar: Each time he writes, he cradles the lightning, and disappears in the conflagration. He is liberated, if temporarily, by each lightning bolt, each flash of *voyance*. No ashes remain: "J'ai été élevé parmi les feux de bois, au bord de braises qui ne finissaient pas cendres" ["I was raised among wood fires, beside embers that did not end as ash"] (CB, 23). What remains is the text, its creator effaced in the act of creation itself, present on the page as luminosity.

But if the lightning in the poplar's poem signifies Char's poetic death, elsewhere it is a metaphor for a much more concrete kind of dying, for Death itself. And yet he always speaks of it with tenderness, even yearning, as in the passage he wrote after he had suffered a stroke in 1968 (several years after the composition of "Effacement du peuplier"):

> Dans la nuit du 3 au 4 mai 1968 la foudre que j'avais si souvent regardée avec envie dans le ciel éclata dans ma tête, m'offrant sur un fond de ténèbres propres à moi le visage aérien de l'éclair emprunté à l'orage le plus matériel qui fût. Je crus que la mort venait, mais une mort où, comblé par une compréhension sans exemple, j'aurais encore un pas à faire avant de m'endormir, d'être rendu éparpillé à l'univers pour toujours. Le chien de coeur n'avait pas geint.
>
> La foudre et le sang, je l'appris, sont un. [NP, 83]

> During the night of May 3-4, 1968, the lightning I'd so often desired from afar burst in my head, presenting against a background of shadows that were mine alone the aerial face of the lightning bolt, borrowed from the most physical storm possible. I thought death was coming, but a death wherein, filled with an unparalleled comprehension, I would still have one more step to take before sleeping, before being scattered to the universe forever. The dog of the heart had not whimpered.
>
> Lightning and blood, I learned, are one.

In fact, Char has always known this, or so it would seem from a reading of his work. Blood and lightning are often coupled in his poems, even his earliest, certainly those written since the war. And it is not a question of blood simply because lightning represents death, but also because it represents the electrifying communication that can occur between two human beings, the encounter that hums along our veins to reach our heart as surely as death does *(tel est le coeur)* and stop it, if only for an instant, to transform us.

Thus in "Affres, détonation, silence," a poem written in memory of a dead comrade who was shot by the Nazis, the deep sense of loss which permeates the beginning of the text is embodied at the end of the text as a lightning bolt—a wandering, electrifying, strangely androgynous creature (for she is clearly a woman, but with the face of a schoolboy) who hungers, as the poet does, for friendship:

> Ne cherchez pas dans la montagne; mais si, à quelques kilomètres de là, dans les gorges d'Oppedette, vous rencontrez la foudre au visage d'écolier, allez à elle, oh, allez à elle et souriez-lui car elle doit avoir faim, faim d'amitié. [FM, 185]

> Don't search on the mountain; but a mile or so away in the Oppedette ravines, if you meet the lightning with a schoolboy face, welcome her, oh! run to welcome her smiling, for she must be hungry, hungry for friendship.

What adds special poignancy to Char's plea is that contact with this lonely lightning bolt, as with all the lightning in his poetry, can kill. "La foudre au visage d'écolier" is the personification of the affection, the human electricity, that once passed between two human beings, but she also symbolizes the destructive electricity, ending in death, between Char's comrade and his executioners—twisted human contact, the encounter violated. She is a mythic entity and an example of "the union of the harmful and the beneficial which characterizes all mythological entities in all human societies. Dionysos is simultaneously 'the most terrible' and 'the most gentle' of all gods. By the same token, there is the Zeus who thunders and the Zeus who is 'sweet as honey.' "[2]

Like the gods and like the melancholy hunter, lightning violently transforms that which it touches. A celestial marksman, it destroys—but preserves essences. It illuminates, it transmutes earth to fire. "La foudre libère l'orage et lui permet de satisfaire nos

plaisirs et nos soifs. Foudre sensuelle!" ["Lightning liberates the
storm and permits it to gratify our pleasures and our thirsts. Sensual
lightning!"] (AC, 12). It liberates the rain, flashing out between two
clouds. It shoots from cloud to earth to send the poplar up in smoke,
but also it leaps between two human beings and their contact lights
the universe, leading to a deeper glimpse of the permanent invisible
than any forest fire can:

ANOUKIS ET PLUS TARD JEANNE

Je te découvrirai à ceux que j'aime, comme un long éclair
de chaleur, aussi inexplicablement que tu t'es montrée à moi,
Jeanne, quand, un matin s'astreignant à ton dessein, tu nous
menas de roc en roc jusqu'à cette fin de soi qu'on appelle un
sommet. Le visage à demi masqué par ton bras replié, les
doigts de ta main sollicitant ton épaule, tu nous offris, au
terme de notre ascension, une ville, les souffrances et la
qualification d'un génie, la surface égarée d'un désert, et le
tournant circonspect d'un fleuve sur la rive duquel des
bâtisseurs s'interrogeaient. Mais je te suis vite revenu,
Faucille, car tu consumais ton offrande. Et ni le temps, ni la
beauté, ni le hasard qui débride le coeur ne pouvaient se
mesurer avec toi.

J'ai ressuscité alors mon antique richesse, notre richesse à
tous, et dominant ce que demain détruira, je me suis souvenu
que tu étais Anoukis l'Étreigneuse, aussi fantastiquement que
tu étais Jeanne, la soeur de mon meilleur ami, et aussi inexplicablement que tu étais l'Étrangère dans l'esprit de ce
misérable carillonneur dont le père répétait autrefois que Van
Gogh était fou.

Saint-Rémy-des-Alpilles, 18 septembre 1949.

[LM, 60]

ANOUKIS AND LATER JEANNE

I will unveil you to those I love, like a long stroke of summer lightning, as inexplicably as you showed yourself to me,
Jeanne, on a morning made to your design when you led us
from rock to rock up to that end of self we call a summit.
Your face half-masked by the arm you bent, the fingers of
your hand seeking your shoulder, you offered us at the end of
our ascent a city, the sufferings and qualifications of a genius,

the scattered surface of a desert, and the circumspect turning
of a river, on whose bank some builders stood questioning.
But quickly I came back to you, my Reaper, for you were
consuming your offering. And neither time nor beauty nor
chance which unbridles the heart could compare with you.

It was then I revived my ancient wealth, the wealth of all
of us, and dominating what tomorrow will destroy, I
remembered you were Anoukis the Clasper, just as incredibly
as you were Jeanne, my best friend's sister, and as inexplicably as you were the Foreigner to that miserable bell-
ringer whose father always used to say Van Gogh was crazy.

Saint-Rémy-des-Alpilles, September 18, 1949

A long flash of lightning, and an act of love ("Je te découvrirai à
ceux que j'aime"), this lovely poem unveils Jeanne, but leaves her
all her mystery. The poet-lover shares with us his sudden vision of
her, but that vision is inexplicable—in two senses. To begin with,
she is herself mysterious. Even in the moment of exposure, when he
sees her truly for the first time, her face remains "à demi masqué,"
and each new name he gives to her, rather than simplifying her identity, enriches it, increases its complexity. She is a sickle, and a goddess, and the sister of his best friend, and a foreigner, all these per-
sonae equally fantastic and finally indecipherable. Recorded,
nonetheless, by "le poète, conservateur des infinis visages du vi-
vant" ["the poet, guardian of the infinite faces of the living"] (FM,
107).

Such multiplicity is typical of all of Char's lovers. They are all
rich with possibilities, with enigmatic metamorphoses: "Tu me
compares continuellement à autrui ou à quelque espèce," remarks
the lover in Char's play *Claire*. "Hier, j'étais un églantier puis une
éphémère, enfin, à la tombée de la nuit un sanglier." "Je n'y peux
rien," *La Rencontrée* replies, "c'est ainsi. Tu n'es jamais celui que
j'ai devant les yeux. Ne proteste pas. C'est cela la richesse!"
["You're always comparing me to someone else or to some other
species. Yesterday I was a dog-rose, then a mayfly, finally when
night fell a wild boar." "I can't help it," the Encountered One
replies, "that's the way it is. You're never the man I have before my
eyes. Don't protest. That is true wealth!"] (TCA, 69). And this is
Jeanne's richness too. Again and again, she is transformed in the
poet's eyes, she is protean, he cannot define her, or perhaps will not:
"Chacun de nous," he writes elsewhere, "peut recevoir / La part
de mystère de l'autre / Sans en répandre le secret" ["Each of us

can contain / The other's share of mystery / Without releasing the secret"] (RBS, 176). What passes between two lovers when they open themselves to each other remains theirs, closed to the outside world like a boxwood shutter, so that their separate mysteries combine as one secret, unified and impenetrable to the rest of us. In "Anoukis" we, like the wretched bell-ringer, will know Jeanne only as the embodiment of mystery—and this despite the extraordinary amount of concrete detail Char gives us in the poem.

But the inexplicability he speaks of in his first line and in his last applies not only to Jeanne herself, but also to his sudden perception of her. That is, why on this particular morning (and let us note that the morning itself is constrained to follow her plan: "quand, un matin s'astreignant à ton dessein. . ."—everything conspires to make him fall in love with her), in this particular setting, as she makes this particular gesture, does he see her? Why did he not see who she was yesterday, why not five minutes from now? The precise moment when one reaches "cette fin de soi qu'on appelle un sommet" is unpredictable. The *coup de foudre* happens; it is a mystery and a cause for rejoicing: "Tout en nous ne devrait être qu'une fête joyeuse quand quelque chose que nous n'avons pas prévu, que nous n'éclairons pas, qui va parler à notre coeur, par ses seuls moyens, s'accomplit" ["Everything in us should be joyous celebration when something we did not foresee, do not attempt to clarify, which is to speak to our heart, all by itself, happens"])LPA, 146). Somehow the lovers work their way to the top of the mountain (Char's lovers are characteristically "on the heights" and it is not always an easy climb), and there they turn and see each other. As we have said, seeing and being seen are inextricably bound up with the Charian dialectic of desire.

What the poet sees on this particular morning is Jeanne's gesture and her "offering," the landscape beneath them, and it is this dual vision that ultimately leads him to call her Anoukis the Clasper. For Anoukis was an Egyptian goddess of the Nile, "she who clasps the river bank and presses the Nile between the rocks of Philae and Syene. She was worshipped at Elephantine with Khnum (god of fecundity and creation) and Sati as a regional goddess of the Cataracts."[3] We have already seen, in connection with "La truite," that waterfalls are often the symbol and setting of passion in Char's poetry, and here he invokes a goddess of the Cataracts whose gesture controls the fertile Nile and keeps it within its banks. (Sati, on the other hand, who is Anoukis' opposite, "lets fly the river's current with the force and rapidity of an arrow."[4]) Jeanne's gesture, described in such detail by the poet—but captured as it ends, so that she is immobilized, a statue, an ancient divinity, her face half-masked, her arm bent, the fingers of one hand nearly touching the opposite shoulder—this gesture makes of her a sickle and duplicates, perhaps, the ancient movement of Anoukis as she gathered in and channeled fruitfully the tumbling waters. And the identification between these two women is further strengthened by the landscape itself, which includes "la surface égarée d'un désert" (Egypt is the land of the desert) and "le tournant circonspect d'un fleuve sur la rive duquel des bâtisseurs s'interrogeaient." Dam-builders perhaps.

But what tumbling waters does Jeanne control? Are they not "le temps. . .la beauté. . .le hasard qui débride le coeur," are they not the poet's heart itself? The gesture with which she points out the landscape, and harvests it, causes the poet to *see* her, to see *her*, and this visionary instant changes everything and unleashes a flood of emotions and images which might overflow, but do not; for they are contained, finally, by the very force of her presence. It is at this moment that she transmits to the poet her own ability to order the chaotic elements of reality, myth, passion, and, above all, time, so that he can *remember* and, remembering, revive the fertile past and "dominate" (like her) the present moment and all the earth around them and all the electricity between them, "ce que demain détruira," to fuse these things in the poem which is her multifaceted portrait. "The oldest of the old follows behind us in our thinking," Heidegger has written, "and yet it comes to meet us. / That is why thinking holds to the coming of what has been, and is remembrance.[5]

Anoukis' husband Khnum "doubtless symbolised the Nile which comes from the heavens to fertilize the earth and make it fruitful."[6] Just so, in Char's text the poet is a river god, his poetry a river, channeled by Jeanne's presence and by her gesture of embrace: the contact between the two of them, which is purely visual, accomplishes an ordering of the universe, both exterior and interior, so that the poet can make his art.

This brings us to Van Gogh, that most Heideggerian of painters.[7] For Char is not the only artist present in the poem. Jeanne points to more than a desert and a river. She points out as well a city and "les souffrances et la qualification d'un génie"—a perplexing phrase until we reach the end of the poem and discover that the city is Saint Rémy, where Van Gogh's genius was qualified as insanity.

Once he is named, even if we had not guessed before, it becomes clear that this poem is as much about art as it is about love. Indeed, the two are inextricable in the text. Jeanne is a controlling creative force: under her hand, the scattered surface of a desert is counterbalanced by the circumspect turning of a river, the former sterile and unruly, like a madman, the latter controlled and fertile, like a brilliant artist, a genius. She sweeps away the immediate, cluttered past and sets the present moment on fire ("Mais je te suis vite revenu, Faucille, car tu consumais ton offrande"), making possible the new and richer resuscitation of the past which is achieved at the end of the poem.

Van Gogh is very much a part of that resuscitation. As much as Anoukis the Clasper, his art belongs to our culture, our communal past, "notre richesse à tous." For as Char writes elsewhere, "il parvient génialement à l'incandescence et à l'inaltéré" ["with his genius he attains incandescence and the inalterable"] (RBS, 36). This incandescent human wealth and our capacity to make it, to create what does not die, remain our central mystery and our highest grace. Char has said he never ceases to be astonished at man's ability, *despite everything* (his emphasis), to reach down inside himself—as does the poet in the course of this poem—and come up with what the poet calls "ce radium" which is Art.[8] This radium, a "long éclair de chaleur," lasts.

As for "ce misérable carillonneur," he is taken from real life,[9] and his insertion into the poem is characteristic of Char and characteristically jolting. For we have been to Egypt and back, we are plunged into mysteries and into the opacity of the human creature, when suddenly the poet confronts us with a wretched bellringer who says Van Gogh was crazy. This, at the end of a text infused with a sense of the sacred, which exalts art and the artist, demonstrates nothing so clearly as the impossibility of defining others in simplistic ways. It is particularly ironic at the end of such a text that Van Gogh the visionary, who truly saw, should himself be seen as a madman.

However, this ending goes further than irony, for as I have suggested, among the poem's themes are vision, the mysteries that defy it—and the sacred. Char identifies his best friend's sister as an ancient goddess, he recognizes that Van Gogh transcends the human condition, is in some sense godlike, and the poet is immensely enriched by these perceptions. In another major poem about poetry, "Le rempart de brindilles" ["The Rampart of Twigs"], Char writes:

Lorsque nous sommes aptes à monter à l'aide de l'échelle
naturelle vers quelque sommet initiant, nous laissons en bas
les échelons du bas; mais quand nous redescendons, nous
faisons glisser avec nous tous les échelons du sommet. Nous
enfouissons ce pinacle dans notre fonds le plus rare et le
mieux défendu, au-dessous de l'échelon dernier, mais avec
plus d'acquisitions et de richesses encore que notre aventure
n'en avait rapporté de l'extrémité de la tremblante échelle.

[LPA, 116-117]

When we are capable of climbing by the natural ladder
toward some initiatory summit, we leave beneath us the lower
rungs; but when we climb back down, we bring along all the
top rungs. We bury this pinnacle in our rarest and best-
defended depths, beneath the bottom rung, but among more
riches and treasure still than our adventure brought back
from the tip of the trembling ladder.

The wretched bell-ringer learns nothing, sees nothing, can only
see that there is something foreign about the poet's companion, just
as his father saw only that there was something odd about the great
painter. And this goes beyond irony. Such blindness is im-
poverishing; it is criminal. "Leur crime: un enragé vouloir de nous
apprendre à mépriser les dieux que nous avons en nous" ["Their
crime: a rabid will to teach us scorn for the gods we have within
us"](LPA, 152).

The whole movement of "Anoukis et plus tard Jeanne" is away
from such contempt, from self-contempt, toward reverence for the
human creature. Here, as elsewhere in Char's work, the human
community is reaffirmed: the poet reaches his visionary instant at
the top of the mountain whose summit is defined as an "end to
self"—an end to the singular, the separate—and he shares his vision
with "those he loves," taking us upwards and backwards into our
communal past, into a time when we had not yet cut ourselves off
from divinity. But let us note too—this too is an affirmation—that
the living woman, Jeanne, is just as wondrous as Anoukis and even
more mysterious to Char, who speaks in another text of "ceux dont
nous disons qu'ils sont des dieux, expression la moins opaque de
nous-mêmes" ["those whom we call gods, the least opaque expression of ourselves"] (NT, 84). The ancient goddess is simpler and for
all her mystery *less opaque* than the actual, present Jeanne, whose

essence slips from us into obscurity. She represents the sudden apparition of the marvelous in everyday life and remains, to the end, as elusive and as deeply desired as the quicksilver trout. And so it can be seen that Char has kept his initial promise: "Je te découvrirai à ceux que j'aime. . .aussi inexplicablement que tu t'es montrée à moi." The unveiling is a mystery, and so is the woman unveiled.

This brings us back to questions of the visible and the invisible in Char's poetry, and to the related themes of proximity and distance: "Je te regarde vivre dans une fête que ma crainte de venir à fin laisse obscure," ["I watch you live in a celebration which my fear of reaching the end leaves dark"], writes the poet in "L'avenir non prédit" ["The Unpredicted Future"] (LPA, 185). What we saw so graphically when we considered hunting—namely, that invisibility and permanence are coupled with each other—is equally true in Char's love poems. In "Les premiers instants," for example: "Adoptés par l'ouvert, poncés jusqu'à l'invisible, nous étions une victoire qui ne prendrait jamais fin" ["Adopted by openness, pumiced to invisibility, we were a triumph that would never end"] (FM, 213). These lovers have disappeared, lightning-struck. They will go on forever. That which is visible perishes in the poet's universe, and, by the same token, proximity kills: the gods die only from being in our midst. Thus, in "Anoukis et plus tard Jeanne" there is necessarily a central core of mystery which remains inviolate, which the poet purposely leaves untouched in his lover, even as he shows her to us. The long flash of lightning that is her poem illuminates her multiplicity and her elusiveness, without giving away her secret.

It is Jean Starobinski who points out that "love's unity is not achieved by a fusion of similar beings, but by asymmetry: our desire as it comes to terms with that portion of unknown and absence within the chance offered which never ceases to elude us. . .An interval must be preserved, we must welcome our chance, our beloved adversary, with all the courtesy due an unknown guest. It cannot be too strongly emphasized that the intensity of the encounter in Char's work is directly linked to our respect for an irreducible distance."[10]

Certainly this is true in the poem we have just been looking at and in "Congé au vent" (Starobinski's example). But the statement implies a kind of *politesse* that is lacking—or that is, in any case, complicated and counterbalanced by violence—in much of Char's love poetry. We have already discussed "Permanent invisible," a text in which the poet himself invokes the word "brutal" to characterize his own love-making. In another of his most celebrated

love poems, "Lettera amorosa," he calls himself a bird of prey,
"mon voeu glacé: saisir ta tête comme un rapace à flanc d'abîme"
["my icy wish: to seize your head like a bird of prey above the
abyss"] (LPA, 96). And it is in the latter poem that he describes love
as guerrilla warfare:

> Je ne puis être et ne veux vivre que dans l'espace et dans
> la liberté de mon amour. Nous ne sommes pas ensemble le
> produit d'une capitulation, ni le motif d'une servitude plus
> déprimante encore. Aussi menons-nous malicieusement l'un
> contre l'autre une guérilla sans reproche. [LPA, 92-93]
>
> ———
>
> I can only be and only wish to live in the space and
> freedom of my love. We two together are not the product of a
> capitulation, nor grounds for an even more depressing ser-
> vitude. Thus we maliciously battle one another in
> reproachless guerrilla warfare.

Total freedom and lack of possessiveness, mutual respect—
nevertheless, even "une guérilla sans reproche" is *warfare*. Polite
perhaps, but dangerous, and every bit as violent as poetry. We have
already said that both are forms of venery. But I think that this particular metaphor, with its chevalric resonance (*le chevalier sans peur
et sans reproche*), leads us to a deep structure in Char's work, and
lights up virtually all the texts we have looked at thus far. For the
creatures that flee through them all behave, in some degree, as does
the guerrilla: freedom is their goal, camouflage their necessity, and
sudden violent contact (lightning) their risk and means of metamorphosis. Char's serpent, his hunter, the women he loves, the warbler
in the reeds, the swift, the amorous lizard, all these are fleeting,
vulnerable, highly mobile creatures who participate in an existence
charged with danger and conflict. The poet stands at the center of
them all, half-hidden, watchful, conscious of his own fragility and of
his own violence; space, liberty, and the unforeseen are his
elements; the lightning bolt his analogue and his ally.
  And there is another character to add to this list, whom we have
not yet discussed: a combative lover, the incomprehensible fighter
in "Le mortel partenaire," whose poem explores the themes of
distance and proximity, physical contact and metaphorical confrontation. Bed, boxing, annihilation, and rebirth are all present in the
following—quite extraordinary—*coup de foudre*:

LE MORTEL PARTENAIRE

Il la défiait, s'avançait vers son coeur, comme un boxeur ourlé, ailé et puissant, bien au centre de la géométrie attaquante et défensive de ses jambes. Il pesait du regard les qualités de l'adversaire qui se contentait de rompre, cantonné entre une virginité agréable et son expérience. Sur la blanche surface où se tenait le combat, tous deux oubliaient les spectateurs inexorables. Dans l'air de juin voltigeait le prénom des fleurs du premier jour de l'été. Enfin une légère grimace courut sur la joue du second et une raie rose s'y dessina. La riposte jaillit sèche et conséquente. Les jarrets soudain comme du linge étendu, l'homme flotta et tituba. Mais les poings en face ne poursuivirent pas leur avantage, renoncèrent à conclure. A présent les têtes meurtries des deux battants dodelinaient l'une contre l'autre. A cet instant le premier dut à dessein prononcer à l'oreille du second des paroles si parfaitement offensantes, ou appropriées, ou énigmatiques, que de celui-ci fila, prompte, totale, précise, une foudre qui coucha net l'incompréhensible combattant.

Certains êtres ont une signification qui nous manque. Qui sont-ils? Leur secret tient au plus profond du secret même de la vie. Ils s'en approchent. Elle les tue. Mais l'avenir qu'ils ont ainsi éveillé d'un murmure, les devinant, les crée. O dédale de l'extrême amour! [LPA, 121-122]

THE MORTAL PARTNER

He challenged her, went straight for her heart, like a boxer—trim, winged, powerful—centered in the offensive and defensive geometry of his legs. His glance weighed the fine points of his adversary who was content to break off fighting, suspended between a pleasant virginity and knowledge of him. On the white surface where the combat was being held, both forgot the inexorable spectators. The given names of the flowers of summer's first day fluttered in the June air. Finally a slight grimace crossed the adversary's cheek and a streak of pink appeared. The riposte flashed back, brusque and to the point. His legs suddenly like linen on the line, the man floated, staggered. But the opposing fists did not pursue their advantage, refusing to conclude the match. Now the two fighters' battered heads nodded against each other. At that instant the first must have purposely pronounced into the second's ear words so perfectly offensive, or appropriate, or enigmatic, that the latter let fly a lightning bolt, abrupt, complete, precise, which knocked the incomprehensible fighter out cold.

Certain beings have a meaning that escapes us. Who are they? Their secret resides in the deepest part of life's own secret. They draw near. Life kills them. But the future they have thus awoken with a murmur, sensing them, creates them. O labyrinth of utmost love!

Here is a classical Charian encounter. Not simply visual, as in "Anoukis et plus tard Jeanne," the lovers' contact in "Le mortel partenaire" is very extensive indeed. Nor do these partners treat each other "with all the courtesy due an unknown guest." Sex is not polite, it is not always gentle. Far from it: "Of eroticism," Georges Bataille has written, "one may say that it is the approbation of life even to the point of death."[11] Bed, which we have already seen as a hunting preserve, becomes here a boxing ring, and the act of making love a confrontation just as violent as the bullfight.

But this "novice corps à corps" is more than a sexual encounter and more than a sports event—otherwise, how explain the poem's mysterious last paragraph? The labyrinth of extreme love evoked by Char is that of the creative act, and his erotic fist fight is an evocation of the poet coming to grips with Poetry. "Nous voici de nouveau seuls en tête à tête, ô Poésie," writes Char. "Ton retour signifie que je dois encore une fois me mesurer avec toi, avec ta juvénile hostilité, avec ta tranquille soif d'espace, et tenir prêt pour ta joie cet inconnu équilibrant dont je dispose" ["Here we are alone again, face to face, O Poetry. Your return means I must once again measure myself against you, against your young hostility, your tranquil thirst for space, and keep ready for your joy that stabilizing unknown which is mine"] (SP, 31).

The poet's passionate boxing match immediately recalls the hunt, and here, as in his bestiary, grammatical gender is rich with meaning and defines to a great extent the behavior of his poetic players. (Nor, let us say in passing, is the lightning itself immune to sexualization in Char's poetic universe. To his "foudre sensuelle," the woman-child we saw in "Effacement du peuplier" and "Affres, détonation, silence"—at times nurturant, at times in need of nurturing—compare the ubiquitous, masculine, Charian *éclair*, as it flashes in and out of his poetry, pointed, spasmodic, in its essence male.) With the very first words of "Le mortel partenaire": "Il la défiait. . . ," we learn that the participants in this drama are a man and a woman. Lovers, perhaps, an impression that is strengthened by the second phrase: "s'avançait vers son coeur." At this point Char introduces his analogy, "comme un boxeur ourlé, ailé et puissant," and his couple is plunged into the heat of battle. But look at how the two of them behave. He (*le poète, le mortel partenaire, l'incompréhensible combattant*) challenges, advances on his adversary, and finally, with a few well-chosen words which we the readers are never privy to, intentionally provokes his own annihilation. The lady in this struggle (*la poésie, la vie elle-même*) is no pacifist, but she does lie back and let him come to her, and it is only after he has delivered his message—perfectly offensive, or appropriate, or enigmatic as it may be—that she knocks him out cold.

We cannot help but pause at Char's characterization of the poem, the enunciation of the poet: offensive, appropriate, enigmatic. Poetry is provocation, a weapon wielded with exactitude; it is also an enigma. And it is fatal to its enunciator, who until the final knockout stands firmly centered in the geometry of his legs, one of Char's many upright men—"Le poète est l'homme de la stabilité unilatérale" ["The poet is a man of unilateral stability"] (FM, 73)—on "la blanche surface," the page. We, then, are the inexorable spectators, whom he forgets in the creative struggle, for he is too busy naming things ("Dans l'air de juin voltigeait le prénom des fleurs du premier jour"). It is only fitting that the pivotal instant in his match be verbal—just as it might be in bed or in an actual boxing match. Two loyal adversaries in the clinch, the poet *speaks*, everything takes fire. So that the end result of the hostilities is an explosion, "prompte, totale, précise, une foudre" which annihilates the poet, and leads to his rebirth, in and through the poem. "From the poem is born the poet," writes Maurice Blanchot[12] (to whom "Le mortel partenaire" is dedicated). "Mon amour," writes Char, "peu importe que je sois né: tu deviens visible à la place où je disparais" ["My love, it matters little that I was born: you become visible in the place I disappear"] (FM, 197).

The poet's self must be effaced, impersonalized ("Modifie-toi, disparais sans regret. . ." ["Change, disappear without regret. . ."] (MSM, 145), torn up and re-begun, to yield that piece of the permanent invisible that is the poem. And if "le mortel partenaire" is incomprehensible, it is because he consents to participate in such a dangerous venture, actively provokes his own erasure. This he does by getting too close to the secret of life itself, which, like all that is truly sacred, kills on contact: "The sacred is always more or less 'that which cannot be approached without dying.' "[13] It is the fighter's proximity, his daring to get near the unapproachable, that destroys him, and illuminates him. He goes forward, like the bull—whose sunstruck, passionate, fatal combat parallels his own—to his undoing, and Char's epithet for him, "incomprehensible," partakes of the same mystery as the bull's epithet, "fascinant," and of the same mystery as Jeanne in all her inexplicability. The river goddess remains intact, however, for she cannot be fully seen. Char's boxer, like his bull, is highly visible, exposed on the white surface of the boxing ring, and he perishes in the desperate nuptial conflict which yields his poem. This is the deepest *coup de foudre* in Char's lexicon, this lightning encounter between the poet and his art, offered to us in its full intensity and joy on the white surface of the page:

> Cette forteresse épanchant la liberté par toutes ses poternes, cette fourche de vapeur qui tient dans l'air un corps d'une envergure prométhéenne que la foudre illumine et évite, c'est le poème, aux caprices exorbitants, qui dans l'instant nous obtient puis s'efface. [FM, 79-80]

> ---

> This fortress pouring freedom from all its posterns, this fork of vapor which holds in the air a body of Promethean breadth, illumined but untouched by lightning, this is the poem, of outrageous whim, which in a flash attains us and is gone.

CHAPTER 5
METEORS

L'écume d'astre coule toute allumée
Il n'y a pas d'absence irremplaçable. [MSM, 71]

The foam of stars flows fully lit
There is no irreplaceable absence.

LIGHTNING SPLITS OPEN THE NIGHT. AND THEN night is reconstituted, within the poet as well as around him. "J'aime qui m'éblouit puis accentue l'obscur à l'intérieur de moi" ["I love the one who dazzles me, then accentuates the dark within"], he writes (LM, 76). Every encounter in his poetic universe is perceived in these terms—love, friendship, warfare, the making of poems, the experience of poetic vision itself:

> La vraie vie, le colosse irrécusable, ne se forme que dans les flancs de la poésie. Cependant l'homme n'a pas la souveraineté (ou n'a plus, ou n'a pas encore) de disposer à discrétion de cette vraie vie, de s'y fertiliser, sauf en de brefs éclairs qui ressemblent à des orgasmes. Et dans les ténèbres qui leur succèdent, grâce à la connaissance que ces éclairs ont apportée, le Temps, entre le vide horrible qu'il sécrète et un espoir-pressentiment qui ne relève que de nous, et n'est que le prochain état d'extrême poésie et de voyance qui s'annonce, le Temps se partagera, s'écoulera, mais à notre profit, moitié verger, moitié désert. [RBS, 127-128]

Real life, the indisputable colossus, is formed only in the flanks of poetry. But man does not have (or no longer has or does not yet have) the sovereignty to dispose at will of this real life, to fertilize himself except in brief lightning bolts that resemble orgasms. And in the shadows following them, thanks to the knowledge these lightning bolts have brought, Time—between the horrible void it secretes and a hope-presentiment which rises only out of us and which is but the coming of the next state of extreme poetry and vision—Time

will parcel itself out, will slip past; but to our profit, half
orchard, half desert.

Real life (poetry) comes as brief lightning bolts. The rest is
shadow and the inexorable movement of Time. But even Time, if it
is half desert, is half orchard too, and the desert part is lit by "a
hope-presentiment," the deeply desired advent of future poems. It
will be seen why waiting, *l'attente*, is so crucial a term, so central an
experience in the poet's universe. Char writes of the woman Poetry:
"Tu es mon amour depuis tant d'années, / Mon vertige devant tant
d'attente, / Que rien ne peut vieillir, froidir. . ." ["You have been
my love so many years, / Vertiginous depths of my waiting, /
That nothing can age or cool. . ."] (RBS, 176). His is a perpetual and
often anguished waiting in the fertile night—"Fertile est la fraîcheur
de cette gardienne!" ["Fertile is the freshness of this guardian!"]
(LM, 168)—for the next illumination, the next flash of lightning. Or
meteor, as the case may be.

Just as the lightning parallels Char's melancholy hunter, so "le
météore du 13 août" is a celestial cousin to his bull and lark, an
ephemeral, sudden presence whose death illuminates: "Etincelle
nomade qui meurt dans son incendie. . ." ["Nomade spark dying in
its fire"] (FM, 204). The meteor's identity is incandescent. Fire is its
voice: "Toute la vertu du ciel d'août, de notre angoisse confidente,
dans la voix d'or du météore" ["All the virtue of the August sky, of
our confiding anguish, in the meteor's voice of gold"] (FM, 148).
This makes it the reverse image of the poet, for his "voix d'encre"
["voice of ink"] (FM, 137) flashes across the whiteness of the page
as does the meteor's tail across the blackness of the night sky, and
for both, as for Char's four fascinating creatures, the instant of
visibility is the instant of death, even as it is the instant of creation.

However, if the meteor's visibility is the sign of its dying, it is
not the cause, for exposure to human eyes is incidental to the fate of
this celestial rock. No hunter is needed to set the meteor on fire, the
very air does that. The meteor gets too close, and it is contact with
Earth's atmosphere, coupled with the rapidity of the fall, that sets it
to burning and renders it, temporarily, visible. If we are fortunate
enough to pick up the fistful of iron which sometimes survives or,
better yet, to see this brief moving drop of light against the sky, it
constitutes a vital message for us, a "chant votif" ["votive song"]
(NT, 62). In the poet's universe, it is a luminous sign of hope, but
hope tempered with pessimism. For the meteor's voyage consumes
it: "Espoir que je tente / La chute me boit" ["Hope I am temp-

ting / My fall drinks me up"] (NP, 68); and it takes its brilliant way across the face of the night.

I would like to look here at two of Char's meteor poems, the first published in 1947, the last published nearly thirty years later.[1]

(1)

"Le météore du 13 août" is one of the poet's long fragmentary texts. It is a "pulverized poem" in form as well as content, dating from the war years, when Char was himself pulverized, torn apart: "La quantité de fragments me déchire" ["The quantity of fragments tears me apart"] (FM, 32). His universe is blown to bits. His art reflects this:

LE MÉTÉORE DU 13 AOÛT

(Le météore du 13 août)

A la seconde où tu m'apparus, mon coeur eut tout le ciel pour l'éclairer. Il fut midi à mon poème. Je sus que l'angoisse dormait.

(Novae)

Premier rayon qui hésite entre l'imprécation du supplice et le magnifique amour.

L'optimisme des philosophies ne nous est plus suffisant.

La lumière du rocher abrite un arbre majeur. Nous avançons vers sa visibilité.

Toujours plus larges fiançailles des regards. La tragédie qui s'élabore jouira même de nos limites.

Le danger nous ôtait toute mélancolie. Nous parlions sans nous regarder. Le temps nous tenait unis. La mort nous évitait.

Alouettes de la nuit, étoiles, qui tournoyez aux sources de l'abandon, soyez progrès aux fronts qui dorment.

J'ai sauté de mon lit bordé d'aubépines. Pieds nus, je parle aux enfants.

(La lune change de jardin)

Où vais-je égarer cette fortune d'excréments qui m'escorte comme une lampe?

Hymnes provisoires! hymnes contredits!

Folles, et, à la nuit, lumières obéissantes.

Orageuse liberté dans les langes de la foudre, sur la souveraineté du vide, aux petites mains de l'homme.

Ne t'étourdis pas de lendemains. Tu regardes l'hiver qui enjambe les plaies et ronge les fenêtres, et, sur le porche de la mort, l'inscrutable torture.

Ceux qui dorment dans la laine, ceux qui courent dans le froid, ceux qui offrent leur médiation, ceux qui ne sont pas ravisseurs faute de mieux, s'accordent avec le météore, ennemi du coq.

Illusoirement, je suis à la fois dans mon âme et hors d'elle, loin devant la vitre et contre la vitre, saxifrage éclaté. Ma convoitise est infinie. Rien ne m'obsède que la vie.

Etincelle nomade qui meurt dans son incendie.

Aime riveraine. Dépense ta vérité. L'herbe qui cache l'or de ton amour ne connaîtra jamais le gel.

Sur cette terre des périls, je m'émerveille de l'idolâtrie de la vie.

Que ma présence qui vous cause énigmatique malaise, haine sans rémission, soit météore dans votre âme.

Un chant d'oiseau surprend la branche du matin.

[FM, 202-204]

THE METEOR OF AUGUST 13TH
(The Meteor of August 13th)

The second you appeared to me, my heart had all the sky to light its way. It was my poem's noon. I knew that anguish slept.

(Novae)

First ray which hesitates between the imprecation of agony and a magnificent love.

Philosophy's optimism is no longer enough.

The rock's light shelters a major tree. We go forward toward its visibility.

Ever deeper wedding of the eyes. The tragedy now unfolding will delight even in our limits.

Danger did away with all our melancholy. We talked without looking at each other. Time held us together. Death avoided us.

Larks of the night, stars, whirling at the wellsprings of abandon, be progress to the brows that sleep.

I have leapt from my hawthorn-bordered bed. Barefoot, I talk to children.

(The Moon Changes Gardens)

Where shall I scatter this treasure of excrement which escorts me like a lamp?

Provisional hymns! Hymns contradicted!

Demented lights, obedient to the night.

Stormy freedom swaddled in lightning, above the sovereignty of the void, in the small hands of man.

Do not lose yourself in tomorrows. You watch winter striding over wounds, gnawing at windows, and, on death's porch, inscrutable torture.

Those who sleep in wool, who run in the cold, who offer their mediation, who are not predators for want of better, are in phase with the meteor, enemy of the cock.

Illusorily, I am both in my soul and outside it, far in front of the windowpane and pressed up against the windowpane, a spilt saxifrage. My lust is infinite. Nothing obsesses me but life.

A nomad spark dying in its fire.

Love a river girl. Spend your truth. The grass which hides your love's gold will never know frost.

On this perilous earth, I marvel at life's idolatry.

May my presence, which causes you enigmatic
uneasiness, unremitting hatred, be a meteor in your soul.

A birdsong surprises the morning's branch.

The richness and complexity of Char's text are dizzying, but it
can immediately be seen to shimmer with hope. "Le météore du 13
août" would come in the middle of the August Perseids, meteoric
showers occurring every August; their hour: after midnight, before
sunrise. Thus, the poet catches sight of his meteor in the middle of
the night, it lights the sky, and when it disappears the first bird is an-
nouncing dawn. Sudden light in the midst of obscurity, which leads
to song: the very definition of poetry itself.

Between the first verse and the last, each a specific moment in
time, and emotion, we are shown a series of novae, invisible stars
that shine quite suddenly, then fade again from view. The verses
constitute a set of self-contained "pensées," illuminations separated
from each other by surrounding space and silence, so that the page
becomes the night sky, strewn with stars—or swept with fragmentary falling fire—a disjointed vision transposed into disjoint song.

The poem's opening section is one verse long—as brief, that is,
and luminous as the meteor whose name it bears, but resonant with
themes that will recur throughout the text:

> A la seconde où tu m'apparus, mon coeur eut tout le ciel
> pour l'éclairer. Il fut midi à mon poème. Je sus que l'angoisse
> dormait.

Among other things, these lines recall the last line of Rimbaud's
"Aube" ["Dawn"]: "Au réveil, il était midi" ["When I awoke it was
noon"]. But Rimbaud's visionary poem starts at dawn and finishes
at noon, with his awakening out of poetry, out of la vraie vie [real
life]. Whereas Char's poem ends with dawn, suggesting that in fact
his poem is about to commence just as he leaves us, and it starts at
noon—although it is this hour only in the poet's heart and in his
poem. The meteor has simulated midday, "the hour of the Greeks,
par excellence," as Georges Mounin has called it, "the hour when
men of solar lands can entertain the idea of death with an objective
serenity."[2] The meteor has temporarily transformed the night into
the day and, doing so, has kindled Char's own "mental light": "La
vraie lumière, celle qui a raison par la particularité et la toute-
puissance de ce qu'elle nomme, de la ténacité du soleil. . . elle relève

doucement le vent qui tombe durant sa course, quand il s'efforce de venir en aide aux hommes dans le désespoir" ["Real light, which, by virtue of the particularity and omnipotence of what it names, gets the better of the sun's tenacity. . . .It softly lifts up the wind when it falls, on its way to help men in despair"] (HW, 214). In Rimbaud's text, the poet sleeps; the poet's anguish sleeps in Char's. And he addresses the creature who has come to illuminate him with that same "tu" we heard him use when speaking to his other masculine allies, the bull and the snake—both of whom his meteor resembles, the former in his burning ("Il ne fait jamais nuit quand tu meurs," says Char of the bull, as well he might of the celestial rock), the latter in his flight into invisibility. All this is expressed in three laconic sentences, dominated by *le passé simple,* a crystallization of the instant Char *saw* and, seeing, wrote "the meteor's votive song."

Novae:
A first uncertain ray of light falls, hesitating between man's curse and his magnificence, his potential for evil and his potential for love, both fulfilled during the war. In his introduction to the second edition of *Le marteau sans maître,* published two years before *Le poème pulvérisé* (and quoted in its entirety in the introduction to this essay), the poet specifically identifies this ray of light as emanating from his own poetry: "La clef du MARTEAU SANS MAÎTRE tourne dans la réalité pressentie des années 1937–1944. Le premier rayon qu'elle délivre hésite entre l'imprécation du supplice et le magnifique amour" ["The key to *The Hammer with No Master* turns in the reality of the years 1937–1944, foreshadowed. The first ray it gives forth hesitates between the imprecation of agony and a magnificent love] (MSM, 13). Faced with these two extremes of human possibility, with "l'hallucinante expérience de l'homme noué au Mal, de l'homme massacré et pourtant victorieux" ["the hallucinating experience of man riveted to evil, of man massacred and still victorious"] (MSM, 13), the poet can only opt for Heraclitean pessimism. Optimism does not suffice:

. . .la seule certitude que nous possédions de la réalité du lendemain, c'est le pessimisme, forme accomplie du secret où nous venons nous rafraîchir, prendre garde et dormir. . . .La perception du fatal, la présence continue du risque, et cette part de l'obscur comme une grande rame plongeant dans les eaux, tiennent l'heure en haleine et nous maintiennent disponibles à sa hauteur. [RBS, 117]

. . .the only certitude we possess of tomorrow's reality is pessimism, perfect form of the secret where we come to renew ourselves, to beware and to sleep. . . . .An awareness of the inevitable, the continual presence of risk, and that portion of darkness like a great oar plunging into the waters, hold time suspended and keep us available at its height.

This statement on pessimism and danger (already quoted, in part, in relation to Char's poplar tree, its vision heightened by the wind which will hasten its own effacement) illuminates the rest of the poet's novae, and the rest of his poetry. He writes: "La lumière du rocher abrite un arbre majeur. Nous nous avançons vers sa visibilité." The meteor's burning gives off tutelary light, exhorts to pessimism, sheltering the tree of knowledge—precisely that "forme accomplie du secret où nous venons nous rafraîchir, prendre garde et dormir." The brilliant effacement of the rock makes danger visible to us, and does so beautifully. It gives us a fleeting, necessary vision of the fatal, of the perpetual presence of risk, and it is this very perception that keeps time suspended, and men (and poplars) "disponibles à sa hauteur."

And this vision weds us to each other ("Toujours plus larges fiançailles des regards. . ."), for we see our common fragility and supply each other with the same perception as the meteor. The realization of our own finitude, our own evanescence, magnifies "la tragédie qui s'élabore"—all of life. In another poem from the same period, also a part of *Le poème pulvérisé*, Char speaks of "vivre, limite immense" ["Living, an immense limit"] (FM, 176): to live is as immense as it is limited. And so the poet ends this section of his poem barefoot, hopeful, calling on the morning stars, "larks of the night," who swirl like a Van Gogh vision at the wellsprings of abandon, to awaken those who still sleep, not yet having shed that hypnotized somnolence ("hypnose") which was the war. "Le créateur est pessimiste, la création ambitieuse, donc optimiste. La rotation de la créature se conforme à leurs prescriptions adverses" ["The creator is pessimistic, the act of creation ambitious, thus optimistic. The creature's rotation complies with their opposing prescriptions"] (RBS, 179).

The moon changes gardens:

We rotate, and the moon shifts. With his play on astrology—moons usually change houses—the poet suggests not only that the war has ended, but also that the whole of this fragmentary text is a horoscope. Indeed, he has written of "Le météore du 13 août":

Les trois phases du météore correspondent aux trois fatalités ou si l'on préfère aux trois directions *contrariées*, en vertu desquelles s'élance, s'ajourne et brûle notre vie, à peu près complètement dépourvue de libre arbitre. Elles traduisent trois états souverains, mais il est impossible d'écrire lequel a plus particulièrement barre sur l'autre, chacun offrant l'illusion d'être le plus profondément, le plus désespérément, le plus allègrement ressenti par nous à l'instar de ses pareils et *presque* à la fois. Dans cette succession de brefs paragraphes nous avons tenté une domification qui ne peut être, hélas, qu'approximative.

———

The three phases of the meteor correspond to the three destinies, or, if you prefer, the three *crossed* ways along which our life shoots, lingers, and burns out, almost completely deprived of free will. These represent three absolute conditions, but it is impossible to say whether one has particular precedence over the other, since each gives the illusion of being the most deeply, the most desperately, the most joyously felt by us, like all the rest and *almost* at the same time. In this series of short paragraphs we have attempted a domification which, alas, can only be approximate. [HW, 208–209. Char's italics]

Jackson Mathews

Men, like meteors, are trapped. Free will has little place in this Heideggerian horoscope—or "domification," as Char calls it (*to domify* meaning to divide into twelve houses, like the zodiac, or the final section of "Le météore," and to specify the position of a planet therein). But it is man's central paradox that he is free and alive only insofar as he perceives his lack of freedom and the brevity of his existence. "Juxtapose à la fatalité la résistance à la fatalité," the poet says elsewhere. "Tu connaîtras d'étranges hauteurs" ["Place alongside fate the resistance to fate. You will know strange heights"] (FM, 188). And then again: "Ma brièveté est sans chaînes. . ." ["My brevity is without chains"] (LPA, 187). This same sense of the poet as a falling, fated creature, only in the instant free, but alive then, and truly fertile, burning with "l'idolâtrie de la vie," lights up the whole last section of "Le météore du 13 août."

This section begins with excrement: "Où vais-je égarer cette fortune d'excréments qui m'escortent comme une lampe?"[3] The poet-meteor is coming out of infertility, on an artistic plane, and deep horror, on a human plane. His "fortune of excrement" is the compost he brings out of this period, and with this compost—which he must scatter, which he must not retain—he will nourish future plants, future poems. In "Feuillets d'Hypnos" he writes:

> Si j'en réchappe, je sais que je devrai rompre avec l'arôme de ces années essentielles, rejeter (non refouler) silencieusement loin de moi mon trésor, me reconduire jusqu'au principe du comportement le plus indigent comme au temps où je me cherchais sans jamais accéder à la prouesse, dans une insatisfaction nue, une connaissance à peine entrevue et une humilité questionneuse. [FM, 137-138]

> _____

> If I escape them, I know I shall have to break with the aroma of these essential years, silently throw away (not repress) my treasure—far away from me—and bring myself back to the principle of the most indigent behavior, as in the period when I sought myself, without ever achieving prowess, in naked dissatisfaction, knowledge scarcely glimpsed and questioning humility.

The reader recognizes as strikingly Charian not only the thought contained within this paragraph—that the *accumulated* experience of the war years must be cast aside, so that the poet may start from scratch, reduced by his own volition to an original naked indigence—but also its rich olfactory imagery. "To break with the aroma of these essential years. . ." Once again we are reminded of "Congé au vent," of the potency of smell therein and the poet's vow to remain mute. The gatherer of mimosas was haloed in her fragrance, her perfume rendered in terms of light. Similarly, in "Le météore du 13 août"—though the image is a good deal more ambiguous—the poet's fortune of excrements escorts him *like a lamp*, or like the luminous tail of the meteor as it moves. As he moves away from war, away from "l'imprécation du supplice," the poet leaves behind his anguish, but it continues to light his way, or rather to signify his passage.

"Le soleil dans l'espace ne vit pas mieux que notre ombre sur terre," Char writes in a much later text, "quelle que soit sa prolixité. Blason déchu, il est seul, nourri de ses excréments; seul comme est seul l'homme. . ." ["The sun out in space does not live any better than our shadow on earth, no matter what its prolixity. Fallen blazon, it is alone, nourished on its excrement; alone as man is alone"] (CB, 32). The poet in "Le météore" is as solitary as the sun, but mobile. This, in contrast to the fixed stars in his poem: "Folles, et, à la nuit, lumières obéissantes." They stay put, they do not move, he does, intoxicated with his newborn freedom—"Orageuse liberté dans les langes de la foudre"—but aware of the sovereignty of the void and the size (so small) of a man's hand.

He is not yet detached, but he is filled with hope and obsessed with life:

> Illusoirement, je suis à la fois dans mon âme et hors
> d'elle, loin devant la vitre et contre la vitre, saxifrage éclaté.
> Ma convoitise est infinie. Rien ne m'obsède que la vie.

The poem is a windowpane and the poet a rock-breaking plant, a saxifrage itself split in two: half of him pressed up against the pane, the other half far into the future, way ahead of himself and of his text.

There are in Char's work always two sides to the mysterious (Mallarméan) windowpane, poetry, "vitre généreuse qui permet parfois, à qui regarde de l'extérieur, d'entrevoir l'habitant du lieu" ["generous pane which sometimes permits the outsider who looks in to glimpse the inhabitant of the place"] (HW, 212–214). And always the poet touches on both sides, is both within and without, as in the following brief poem:

LE CARREAU

Pures pluies, femmes attendues,
La face que vous essuyez,
De verre voué aux tourments,
Est la face du révolté;
L'autre, la vitre de l'heureux,
Frisonne devant le feu de bois.

Je vous aime mystères jumeaux,
Je touche à chacun de vous;
J'ai mal et je suis léger.
[LM, 52]

THE WINDOWPANE

Pure rains, awaited women,
The face you bathe,
Of glass doomed to torment,

Is the face of the rebel;
The other, the happy windowpane,
Shivers before the wood fire.

I love you, twin mysteries,
I touch upon each of you;
I hurt and I am weightless.

The masculine *carreau*, turned outward and tormented, bathed by feminine, long-awaited rains, and the feminine *vitre*, which turns inward to shiver before the masculine fire, represent twin mysteries, the two sides of the poet's sensibility, which touch and marry in the two-sided transparency, his poem.

But in "Le météore du 13 août" the poet's dual nature is further imaged as a divided saxifrage, and this too has reverberations elsewhere in his work, most notably in "Partage formel"—"Fureur et mystère tour à tour le séduisirent et le consumèrent. Puis vint l'année qui acheva son agonie de saxifrage" ["Furor and mystery by turns seduced and consumed him. Then came the year which put an end to his saxifrage agony"] (FM, 68)—and in a text entitled "Pour un Prométhée saxifrage" ["For a Promethean Saxifrage"], which evokes Hölderlin and ends with the following promise:

> Noble semence, guerre et faveur de mon prochain, devant la sourde aurore je te garde avec mon quignon, attendant ce jour prévu de haute pluie, de limon vert, qui viendra pour les brûlants, et pour les obstinés. [LPA, 177]

> Noble sowing, my neighbor's war and favor, before the muted dawn I keep watch over you along with my hunk of bread, waiting for the day I foresee of tall rain, of green loam, which will come for those who burn, and those who persist.

Meteoric flame and obstinate fragility combine in the poet, who is a Promethean saxifrage, chained to the rock for having stolen fire from the gods, but growing in that rock. *La lumière du rocher abrite un arbre majeur.* He is a stubborn plant and a nomadic spark as well, who urges his reader in "Le météore" to love a river girl (rivers move), to spend himself, here, now, "on this earth of perils," the poet-meteor's last wish: "Que ma présence qui vous cause énigmatique malaise, haine sans rémission, soit météore dans votre âme."

He does not want to reassure us. What he offers, like the hunter and the sprightly snake, is disruption, deep uneasiness, and an instant of illumination.

Suddenly it is dawn, the hour of the lark, the hour when *les Matinaux* awake: "Un chant d'oiseau surprend la branche du matin." We are still in the garden, but the meteor is gone, its poem left behind to shine and sing. This dawn, like others, signifies a break with what preceded it, here with the hypnosis that was war. But if the world at large has been asleep, this is not so of the poet. He has been standing sentry duty in the "knotty night" ("Porteront rameaux ceux dont l'endurance sait user la nuit noueuse qui précède et suit l'éclair. Leur parole reçoit existence du fruit intermittent qui la propage en se dilacérant. . ." ["They will bear palms, whose endurance has learned to consume the gnarled night which precedes and follows the lightning bolt. Their speech takes existence from the intermittent fruit which propagates it by tearing itself apart"] (NP, 31)—and so saw the meteor, the source and symbol of his fiery hope.

Char tells us at the outset that his anguish has been put to sleep. Nonetheless "Le météore" remains a bumpy, anguished poem, whose often violent vocabulary and fragmented form are meant to jolt the reader, and do. Despite the poet's affirmation of life, his text is permeated with a sense of suffering and deep pessimism, and armed with words like agony, imprecation, punishment, tragedy, excrement, wounds, inscrutable torture. These leap out at us, and at the end of the poem, as we have seen, the poet makes his adversary stance explicit: he wishes to provoke his reader, and his very presence causes us "unremitting hatred." Poetry becomes warfare. Still mysterious, but very different from the tender mystery of "Anoukis et plus tard Jeanne," Char's meteoric verses are projectiles—bullets, cosmic rocks, lightning bolts—compressed, hermetic, Heraclitean, encased in silence resembling those infinite spaces whose child the meteor is.

Yet still, no matter how aggressive, Char's "Météore du 13 août" mirrors the human condition and links us, for the brevity of its burning, to the cosmos, for:

l'homme, n'est-ce pas, n'est qu'un excès de matière solaire, avec une ombre de libre arbitre comme dard. Sur un cratère d'horreurs et sous la nuit imbécile s'épanouit soudain, au niveau de ses narines et de ses yeux, la fleur réfractaire, la nova écumante, dont le pollen va se mêler, un pur moment, à

son esprit auquel ne suffisaient pas l'intelligence terrestre
argutieuse et les usages du ciel. [RBS, 46]

---

isn't man only a little excess solar matter, shadowed with a
dart of free will? Above a crater of horrors and beneath the
imbecile night there suddenly blooms, at the level of his
nostrils and his eyes, the refractory flower, the foaming nova,
whose pollen will mix for one pure moment with his mind, for
which neither earth's quibbling intelligence nor the habits of
the sky sufficed.

We are solar matter, "des météores à gueule de planète"
["planet-faced meteors"], slower to burn and disappear than the
frothing nova, the drop of light that we watch for and sometimes
catch a glimpse of in the imbecile night, but quicker to burn
ourselves out than still another kind of meteor, the poem. Its fire is
incorruptible. It outlasts us all, shooting stars, human beings (even
poets), brook trout. It bursts into flame—but invisible flame, for the
substance of poetry is "cet absolu inextinguible, ce rameau du
premier soleil: le feu non vu, indécomposable" ["that inex-
tinguishable absolute, that branch of the first sun: unseen fire, in-
decomposable"] (FM, 68). Sung fire, the poetic meteor crosses our
internal field of vision, our mind's eye, and burns there, luminous
and mobile, yet immobilized, suspended, caught forever at the
highest point of its incendiary voyage, in a perpetual state of becom-
ing, le désir demeuré désir.

(2)

Thirty years after the meteor of the 13th of August has fur-
rowed the page with light, Char's "Évadé d'archipel" ["Escaped
from the Archipelago"], Orion, falls back down among us.
Pigmented with the infinite and with a thirst for the earth, his
features blackened by his meteoric voyage, he likes it here and
stays, setting the stars he has deserted whispering (AC, 9). As was
suggested earlier, in this figure out of Greek mythology (and out of
the sky above Char's house), who unlike Hippolytus not only hunts
but is a ladies' man as well—participating, that is to say, in two different forms of venery with equal ardor—blinded by his first love's
father, loved then by Diana, goddess of the hunt, accidentally killed
by her and flung up to the heavens as a constellation, Char has found
a cluster of stars with human outline for a mirror and companion, a

figure who picks up the threads of many of the themes and images we have been looking at. Orion is a solitary traveler, but he builds bridges for the rest of us and thus combines his solitude with solidarity: "Orion, charpentier de l'acier? Oui, lui toujours; et vers nous" ["Orion, carpenter of steel? Yes, him always; and towards us"] (AC, 37). He dwells in both spheres of the cosmos, celestial and terrestrial. He is a hunter, though a sightless older hunter now, himself a prey to bees and flowers, and vulnerable to the fragrance of the earth:

RÉCEPTION D'ORION

Qui cherchez-vous brunes abeilles
Dans la lavande qui s'éveille?
Passe votre roi serviteur.
Il est aveugle et s'éparpille.
Chasseur il fuit
Les fleurs qui le poursuivent.
Il tend son arc et chaque bête brille.
Haute est sa nuit; flèches risquez vos chances.

Un météore humain a la terre pour miel.

[AC, 27]

ORION'S RECEPTION

Dark bees, whom are you seeking
In the lavender awaking?
Your servant king is passing by.
Blind, he strays, dispersing.
A hunter, he flees
The flowers pursuing him.
He bends his bow and each creature shines.
High is his night; arrows take your chance.

A human meteor has the earth for honey.

Mary Ann Caws

In the awakening lavender the brown bees seek someone—as raw material for their honey?—perhaps the scattered substance of their keeper, Orion, their "servant king" himself. He is blind and scattering, pursued, a meteor against his own high night, but he remains a hunter. He has but to bend his bow and each beast shines. Even if he cannot see, it is the gesture of the hunter that illuminates.

His arrows fly toward their risk (*theirs*), their arced flight mimicking the meteor's.

A white line of ellipsis intervenes. ("Cette extension presque intolérable entre le souffle consentant et le pas hésitant. Doucir l'obstacle. Après la chute interminable, nous gisons écrasés sur le sol. Nous continuons à vivre et à apprendre" ["That almost intolerable stretch between the consenting breath and the hesitant step. The obstacle must be softened. After the interminable fall, we lie crushed on the earth. We continue to live and to learn"] [AC, 21].)

Then the alexandrine: A human meteor has the earth for honey. A verse which stands out from the others in its syllabification, placement within the space of the page and lack of rhyme. An abrupt proverb, a meteorite hitting home. The "dried-up moon" (CB, 66) has been left behind, the fleeting human creature marries earth (lavender, bees, shining unseen beasts, his honeyearth), "Terre d'oubli, terre prochaine, dont on s'éprend avec effroi. Et l'effroi est passé. . ." ["Earth of forgetfulness, close earth we fall in love with fearfully. And the fear is past. . ."] (AC, 10).

In *From Honey to Ashes*, Lévi-Strauss has spoken at length of the profound connections in myth between the substance of honey, "which radiates ambiguity in all its aspects"[4]—being sometimes sweet and highly valued as food, sometimes poisonous—and certain heavenly bodies, namely, the Pleiades and Orion. The Pleiades, Lévi-Strauss notes, like honey, "are ambivalent and may be both desired and feared."[5] We can see that in Char's Orion poems this same ambiguity attaches to the planet Earth, which is the human meteor's honey, desired, feared, by turns life-giving and death-dealing, partaking of the natural and of the sacred.

Orion's honey spins at the center of the sexualized Charian cosmos. Feminine flowers and feminine bees are paired with the masculine hunter, the masculine meteor wedded to feminine earth. In this, the poem echoes many earlier texts, as well as in its evocation of the bee, who elsewhere symbolizes fertile violence (FM, 211) and the farthest of frontiers: "Elle transporte le verbe, l'abeille frontalière qui, à travers haines ou embuscades, va pondre son miel sur la passade d'un nuage" ["She transports the word, does the borderer bee who, past hates and ambushes, goes to lay her honey on the passing fancy of a cloud"] (LPA, 132). The "ambient bee" (FM, 171) is a great traveler. Always a partner to the rooted flower, just as the bird is partner to the rooted tree, the bee pollinates, transporting words—the scattered substance of the poet—from poem to poem. Although feminine, she is a pointed creature, like the serpent with whom she is associated (RBS, 180); her métier is a "métier de pointe." Orion as beekeeper is as apt a stand-in for the poet as Orion-hunter.

Nor is his blindness incidental to his close relationship with bees and flowers. "*We are the bees of the invisible,*" wrote Rilke, of poets.[6] Here is a text by Char:

L'UNE ET L'AUTRE

Qu'as-tu à te balancer sans fin, rosier, par longue pluie, avec
    ta double rose?
Comme deux guêpes mûres elles restent sans vol.
Je les vois de mon coeur car mes yeux sont fermés.
Mon amour au-dessus des fleurs n'a laissé que vent et nuage.

                    [LPA, 166]

———

ONE AND THE OTHER

Why do you poise there endlessly, rose-bush, under long rain,
    with your double rose?
Like two ripe wasps they remain, flightless.
I see them with my heart for my eyes are closed.
My love has left only wind and cloud above the flowers.

Here two roses metamorphose into "ripe wasps," immobilized (unlike their sister the mobile bee), invisible—yet seen by the lover/poet's heart, the organ of truest vision, according to Heidegger.[7] Fleetingly, these flowers recall the heart-like swift, whom no eyes could hold. But the swift was present as a cry, and it was speed that rendered him invisible, whereas the double rose in "L'une et l'autre" is silent, fragrant, and invisible only because the poet has closed his eyes, to make its blossoms disappear, to make them—like his absent lover—into memories, remembered flowers, whose image penetrates directly to the poet's heart.

Orion is sightless. Anything he sees will be seen internally. Externally he is dependent on his other senses, most especially his sense of smell. This and the aromatic herbs around him will guide his hunt. Unlike his forerunner the melancholy hunter, he will set no forest fires, although the mere gesture of tightening his bowstring gives off light. Quite the contrary, he is the one who risks being set on fire:

FRONT DE LA ROSE

Malgré la fenêtre ouverte dans la chambre au long congé, l'arôme de la rose reste lié au souffle qui fut là. Nous sommes une fois encore sans expérience antérieure, nouveaux venus, épris. La rose! Le champ de ses allées éventerait même la hardiesse de la mort. Nulle grille qui s'oppose. Le désir resurgit, mal de nos fronts évaporés.

Celui qui marche sur la terre des pluies n'a rien à redouter de l'épine, dans les lieux finis ou hostiles. Mais s'il s'arrête et se recueille, malheur à lui! Blessé au vif, il vole en cendres, archer repris par la beauté. [LPA, 123]

BROW OF THE ROSE

Despite the window open in the room of long leave, the rose fragrance remains joined to the breath which was there. Once again we are without prior experience, newcomers, in love. The rose! The field of its moving paths would fan away even death's boldness. No gate to make opposition. Desire surges up afresh, disorder of our flighty foreheads.

He who walks on the earth of rains has nothing to fear from the thorn, in places finite or hostile. But should he stop to meditate, woe to him! Wounded to the quick, he flies to ashes, archer recaptured by beauty.

Mary Ann Caws

The scent of the rose is stronger than death itself in this text. No gate can keep it out. It effaces all prior experience and causes the very foreheads of the lovers to evaporate in desire. It is as potent a force as the waterfall in "Les premiers instants" (FM, 213), which pumices its lovers to invisibility. Thorns are not to be feared. It is pure beauty, in the form of fragrance, that strikes the archer like a lightning bolt (or arrow) so that he flames and flies in ashes. As in "Evadé d'archipel" where, "blind, he strays dispersing. / A hunter, he flees / The flowers pursuing him."

The hunter-meteor and his earthly twin the poet, "deux laboureurs aveugles" ["two blind laborers"] (AC, 40), are pursued by scents. We begin to understand the title of Orion's book. The poet has said it is a work of age,[8] and certainly we feel the presence of death—it hovers like a smell—repeatedly in *Aromates chasseurs*.

This and Beauty, but a beauty about to be lost, are the pursuers. In
the title poem, for example, which ends: "Nous ne sommes plus
dans l'incurvé. Ce qui nous écartera de l'usage est déjà en chemin.
Puis nous deviendrons terre, nous deviendrons soif" ["We are no
longer in the concave. That which will take us out of use is already
on the way. Then we will become earth, we will become thirst"]
(AC, 12–13).

Orion takes his leave of his fellow constellations in the first part
of the book; the following poems are a hymn, not unambivalent, to
earth; and at the last the celestial hunter speaks the poet's own fare-
well for him:

ÉLOQUENCE D'ORION

Tu te ronges d'appartenir à un peuple mangeur de
chevaux, esprit et estomac mitoyens. Son bruit se perd dans
les avoines rouges de l'événement dépouillé de son grain de
pointe. Il te fut prêté de dire une fois à la belle, à la sour-
cilleuse distance les chants matinaux de la rébellion. Métal
rallumé sans cesse de ton chagrin, ils me parvenaient humides
d'inclémence et d'amour.

Et à present si tu avais pouvoir de dire l'aromate de ton
monde profond, tu rappellerais l'armoise. Appel au signe vaut
défi. Tu t'établirais dans ta page, sur les bords d'un ruisseau,
comme l'ambre gris sur le varech échoué; puis, la nuit
montée, tu t'éloignerais des habitants insatisfaits, pour un
oubli servant d'étoile. Tu n'entendrais plus geindre tes
souliers entrouverts. [AC, 43]

ORION'S ELOQUENCE

It gnaws at you to belong to a horse-eating people whose
spirit and stomach adjoin. Their noise disperses amidst the
red oats of the event stripped of its pointed grain. Once it was
given you to speak the matinal songs of rebellion to beautiful,
to haughty distance. Metal ceaselessly rekindled of your sor-
row, they reached me humid with inclemency and love.

And at present were you able to name the aromatic herb
of your deep world, you would recall artemisia. Appeal to the
sign is as good as defiance. You would establish yourself in
your page, on the edge of a brook, like ambergris washed up
on seaweed. Then, the night risen, you would withdraw from

the dissatisfied inhabitants, to go toward an oblivion which would serve you as a star. You would no longer hear the moaning of your half-open shoes.

In this destitute time, to the poet's torment, men eat horses rather than honor them as beautiful and noble beasts. Whereas once they hungered for secret meat, for the illuminative death of the sun-bull, piercing, now the pointedness—the penetrating, lightning-like moment of truth, "son grain de pointe"—has gone out of the event (a term recalling Heidegger's illuminating "Ereignis"). What was once given, on loan, to the poet, the rebellious matinal songs he offered up to a Distance as haughty and beautiful and coldly feminine as Baudelaire's "Beauté," is finished. Forged of the constantly rekindled metal of the poet's suffering, but humid with love and inclemency (the image is of a blacksmith, plunging the molten horseshoe, perhaps, into a cooling turbulence of water), these songs rose to where Orion waited. How else explain the odd change of personal pronoun in the last line of the first paragraph? Who is the suddenly, subtly present *I* in this text—Orion, or Poetry herself perhaps? Whoever, whatever second identity we may ascribe to the indirect personal pronoun *me*, clearly it is a part of the poet himself, as is the "tu" of the poem. Spoken with the eloquence of Orion, with his meteoric "voix d'or," the text remains a communication from and to the poet—whose powers seem to be at best problematic: his second paragraph exists entirely in the conditional.

And yet. . ."Appel au signe vaut défi." To write is to resist. The sign is equal to the act, and the poet's use of paraleipsis, his speculation as to what he would invoke, had he sufficient power to name the aromatic herb which corresponds to his deep world, gives him sufficient power to invoke "armoise." The fragrant herb of Artemis, goddess of the hunt and of fertility, its first syllable deeply resonant (in French, "ar" is pronounced exactly like "art"), and recalling Char's own Artine.

What is of special interest is that, in his seeming impotence, it is a fragrant plant—a smell—the poet conjures to represent and thus restore to him his inner world. We have already commented on the potency of fragrance, which can kill, and suggested that it is the smell of his own death the poet flees from in *Aromates chasseurs*. Yet artemisia comes to fortify him here, to stand for him. Let us go back to Char's observation, quoted at the end of "Le météore du 13 août":

L'homme, n'est-ce pas, n'est qu'un excès de matière solaire, avec une ombre de libre arbitre comme dard. Sur un cratère d'horreurs et sous la nuit imbécile s'épanouit soudain, *au niveau de ses narines* et de ses yeux, *la fleur réfractaire*, la nova écumante, dont le pollen va se mêler, un pur moment, à son esprit auquel ne suffisaient pas l'intelligence terrestre argutieuse et les usages du ciel. [RBS, 46. My italics]

For isn't man only a little excess solar matter, shadowed with a dart of free will? Above a crater of horrors and beneath the imbecile night there suddenly blooms, *at the level of his nostrils* and his eyes, *the refractory flower*, the foaming nova, whose pollen will mix for one pure moment with his mind, for which neither earth's quibbling intelligence nor the uses of the sky sufficed.

The fragrance of the stubborn flower is as startling, abrupt and fertile, as illuminating as the sudden flashing of a hitherto invisible star. In fact, the two are equivalent, one coming from the heavens to sustain us as a vision, the other rising from the earth to nurture and enrich us at the level of our nostrils.

Thus, in the second paragraph of "Eloquence d'Orion," the poet summons artemisia as his ally, his defiant deepest sign, and he goes on to spin out further his olfactory image: "Tu t'établirais dans ta page, sur les bords d'un ruisseau, comme l'ambre gris sur le varech échoué. . ." Ambergris is a morbid secretion from the intestine of the sperm whale. It is found floating on the surface of the sea. There it is gathered, its essence being highly valued in the making of perfume.[9]

When night has risen and the poet has withdrawn, oblivious at last to the plaint of his open shoes, what will remain behind on the page is ambergris: the poet's inner world—his flesh and blood mortality, as well as his less grossly physical self: thought, fantasy, desire—refined to a scent, an essence, poetry, the fragrant invisible trace of the poet's passage. ("Temps, mon possédant et mon hôte, à qui offres-tu, s'il en est, les jours heureux de tes fontaines? A celui qui vient en secret, avec son odeur fauve, les vivre auprès de toi, sans fausseté, et pourtant trahi par ses plaies irréparables?" ["Time, my possessor and my host, to whom, if anyone, do you offer the happy days of your fountains? To the one who comes in secret, with his untamed odor, to live them near you, without falsity, and yet betrayed by his irreparable wounds?"] [NP, 104].)

CHAPTER 6
POEMS AND
THE POET

Au silence de celle qui laisse rêveur.

[MSM. 39]

To the silence of the one who leaves us dreaming.

CHAR HAS WRITTEN—AND BEEN SO QUOTED IN THE
first pages of this essay, this hunt—"Un poète doit laisser des traces
de son passage, non des preuves. Seules les traces font rêver" ["A
poet must leave traces of his passage, not proofs. Only traces make
us dream"] (LPA, 153). As one of Derrida's English translators comments, in speaking of the Derridean *trace*, "the reader must remind
himself of at least the track, even the spoor, contained within the
French word."[1] We have throughout these pages been tracking the
poet, been on the poet's trail throughout his own pages, following
"mon errance endurcie" ["my hardened wandering"] (CB, 11): his
poems. And he, meanwhile, has been ahead of us, invisible. Nor will
he stop. "Nous marcherons, nous marcherons, nous exerçant encore
à une borne injustifiable à distance heureuse de nous. Nos traces
prennent langue" ["We will march on, we will march on, testing
ourselves against an unjustifiable limit at exactly the right distance
from us. Our traces start to speak"] (NT, 58). His traces signify the
poet's passing through, and they change, fruitfully, over time:

VÉTÉRANCE

Maintenant que les apparences trompeuses, les miroirs pi-
quetés se multiplient devant les yeux, nos traces passées de-
viennent véridiquement les sites où nous nous sommes
agenouillés pour boire. Un temps immense, nous n'avons cir-
culé et saigné que pour capter les traits d'une aventure commune. Voici que dans le vent brutal nos signes passagers
trouvent, sous l'humus, la réalité de ces poudreuses en-
jambées qui lèvent un printemps derrière elles. [NT, 80]

VETERANCE

Now that deceptive appearances, all the pockmarked mirrors, are multiplying before our eyes, our past traces truly become the sites where we have knelt to drink. For an immeasurable time we moved about and bled only to capture the features of a common adventure. And so in the brutal wind our passing signs find the reality, beneath the humus, of those powdery strides which stir up spring behind them.

In this text from *La nuit talismanique*, the poet's "trace"—the mark of his passage and of his absence—is transmuted into a "site," a rich term in the Charian vocabulary, always a special setting, here a fertile former watering place which only now can be perceived as truly having been such. What lends to the site its truth, its reality, is the proliferation in the destitute present of falsehood, false appearances, "pockmarked mirrors" (an image suggesting, among other things, those mirrors set to trap the lark and lead her to her death). If the veteran in this text has bled and "circulated" in order to capture the essence of our common humanity, the poem tells us he has won. For his passing signs, his poems, locate, underneath the humus, the reality of springtime—or, more exactly, the reality of his past powdery strides which give rise now to spring, having kicked it up behind them in their wake. Movement is fertile, is poetry. And poetry founds the site—which for Char, in his conversation as in his art, is that specially prepared, specially created space wherein "la fête," a celebration, can occur, a space set aside for man, or *chosen* by him, at the center of a hostile universe and the center of his own measured-out mortality, a place wherein his "malédiction" lies, for one suspended moment, dormant, as at the end of "Nous avons": "Un mystère plus fort que leur malédiction innocentant leur coeur, ils plantèrent un arbre dans le Temps, s'endormirent au pied, et le Temps se fit aimant" ["A mystery stronger than their curse clearing their hearts of blame, they planted a tree in Time, fell asleep beneath it, and Time grew loving"] (LPA, 195). Time ceases to be hostile here, it becomes a synonym for earth and both together form men's natural site, a magnet, holding them, lovingly.

In private conversation Char speaks of the "giants" who peopled his childhood, men like the mower who would set out for work an hour early in order to find the site, the place of beauty and repose, where he could later stop to take his lunch.[2] Orion is of their race, in love with earth, which others today are destroying: "Une

terre qui était belle a commencé son agonie, sous le regard de ses
soeurs voltigeantes, en présence de ses fils insensés" ["Earth which
was beautiful has gone into its death throes, beneath the gaze of its
sister acrobats, in the presence of its senseless sons"] (LPA, 194).
We destroy the earth to build underground missile silos. The poet
protests: "Que les perceurs de la noble écorce terrestre d'Albion
mesurent bien ceci: nous nous battons pour un *site* où la neige n'est
pas seulement la louve de l'hiver mais aussi l'aulne du
printemps. . . .A nos yeux ce *site* vaut mieux que notre pain, car il ne
peut être, lui, remplacé" ["Let the piercers of the noble terrestrial
crust of Albion measure this well: we are fighting for a *site* where
the snow is not simply the wolf of winter but also the alder of
spring. . . .In our eyes this *site* is worth more than our bread, for
unlike the latter it cannot be replaced."] (NP, 74; Char's italics). The
silos are built nonetheless. Only the page retains—remains—the site.

POUR RENOUER

Nous nous sommes soudain trop approchés de quelque
chose dont on nous tenait à une distance mystérieusement
favorable et mesurée. Depuis lors, c'est le rongement. Notre
appuie-tête a disparu.

Il est insupportable de se sentir part solidaire et im-
puissante d'une beauté en train de mourir par la faute
d'autrui. Solidaire dans sa poitrine et impuissant dans le
mouvement de son esprit.

Si ce que je te montre et ce que je te donne te semblent
moindres que ce que je te cache, ma balance est pauvre, ma
glane est sans vertu.

Tu es reposoir d'obscurité sur ma face trop offerte,
poème. Ma splendeur et ma souffrance se sont glissées entre
les deux.

Jeter bas l'existence laidement accumulée et retrouver le
regard qui l'aima assez à son début pour en étaler le fonde-
ment. Ce qui me reste à vivre est dans cet assaut, dans ce
frisson. [LPA, 134]

TO RESUME

We suddenly got too close to something from which we'd
been kept at a mysteriously favorable and measured distance.
Since then, corrosion. Our headrest has disappeared.

It is unbearable to feel oneself a committed and impotent part of a beauty dying through the fault of others. Committed in one's breast and impotent in the movement of one's mind.

If what I show you and what I give you seem less to you than what I hide, my weighing is poor, my reaping ineffectual.

You are, poem, a wayside altar of darkness on my too-exposed face. My splendor and my suffering have slipped between the two.

I must cast off life's ugly accumulation and find again the gaze that loved it enough in the beginning to display its foundation. What is left for me to live exists in this assault, this tremor.

Limpid and elliptical, this lovely text speaks with direct obliquity—openly veiled—to questions raised many pages ago: how distant must the poet and the reader be, from one another, from the world rendered visible (how much?) within the text? This is the issue of artistic exposure, how much does the poet allow us to see, what does he show, what withhold, and why. (". . .Comment délivrer la poésie de ses oppresseurs? La poésie qui est clarté énigmatique et hâte d'accourir, en les découvrant, les annule" ["How to save poetry from its oppressors? By uncovering them, poetry—which is enigmatic clarity and eager headlong running—does away with them."] [RBS, 151].)

Remarkably mobile in these five brief stanzas, Char slips in and out of five distinct grammatical persons: first person plural (he opens with an observation on the contemporary human condition, being-in-the-world as it is today, or was in 1962, when *La parole en archipel* first appeared); third person singular (how "one" feels about the threatened beauty of the earth); first person singular (the poet comes out of hiding—does he?); second person singular ("tu" is the poem, directly addressed); and, finally, a kind of generalized third person imperative, which the poet applies most particularly to himself. As we have seen, movement is fertile, is poetry. Here, the mobility of the text joins with speech as simple and mysterious as water. No knot of iron, this poem, as was "le météore"—although there is a knot in the title—but rather, a veil, woven by the poet to protect the beauty and the mystery he sees dying at the hands of others, and woven to protect himself, revealing and concealing him in the same moment, the perfect expression of his own ambivalence.

We have suddenly got too close to "something"—first veil: he will not identify what we have approached so fatally, and this refusal reestablishes, at least within the text, the mysteriously favorable and measured distance whose loss he mourns. Once this distance is gone, corrosion sets in, the slow dying, the corruption of all forms of life that we have seen to grieve the poet throughout his work. He writes in *Aromates chasseurs*: "Ronger est l'un des rares verbes qui puisse se conjuguer par une complète obscurité. Quelle excellence sous le travail empressé de la dent! Et comme l'objet ainsi pelé a lieu de se féliciter! Il ronronne de contentement. Ronger c'est ritualiser la mort" ["To gnaw is one of those rare verbs that can be conjugated by a complete darkness. What excellence beneath the tooth's zealous work! And how the object thus stripped has grounds for self-congratulation. It purrs with contentment. To gnaw is to ritualize death"] (AC, 20).

"Our headrest has disappeared." Laconic, suddenly concrete, the doubly metonymic image jolts, but illuminates. For we have nowhere to lean our heads, no way of knowing where to place them, how much distance to establish between our eyes, our minds, and that *something* our proximity corrodes. It is with our heads—or what is inside them (here is the metonymy within the metonymy), the intellect—that we have set the destructive process in motion. Like Heidegger,[3] Char deplores the technological mind which turns the earth into an object to be regulated, willed, which strips away all mystery, or attempts to, as did the *carillonneur* at the end of "Anoukis et plus tard Jeanne." Char writes: "La science ne peut fournir à l'homme dévasté qu'un phare aveugle, une arme de détresse, des outils sans légende. Au plus dément: le sifflet de manoeuvres" ["Science can only furnish devastated man with a blind lighthouse, a weapon of distress, tools without legend. At its most demented: the whistle of maneuvers"] (NP, 87).

Science is blind. What truly sees is the heart, which has its reasons that Reason does not know—a Pascalian dichotomy articulated in the second stanza of "Pour renouer," wherein the poet states his solidarity (and states it in another metonymy—obliquely, that is to say) with the dying beauty that his mind is impotent to save. The heart's domain is poetry, and poetry can capture beauty without killing it. The poet can reconstitute a saving distance, in fact has done so since his opening sentence, but the line he treads, "la ligne hermétique de partage de l'ombre et de la lumière" ["the hermetic line separating shadow and light"] (LPA, 196), is delicate. To reinstate the mystery he seeks, ellipsis must be counterbalanced with explicitness. The poet risks leaving too much out:

Si ce que je montre et ce que je te donne te semblent
moindres que ce que je te cache, ma balance est pauvre, ma
glane est sans vertu.

Poetry refines the poet's inner world and the world he sees
around him. It gleans, weighs. The poet's constant question: how
much do I show? Or, perhaps, how much *can* I show? How much will
language bear—bare—and I myself? In an early poem, dating from
Char's Surrealist period, he writes: "Les amants. . .flétrirent le
crime passionnel, rendirent le viol au hasard, multiplièrent l'attentat
à la pudeur, sources authentiques de la poésie" ["The lovers
stigmatized crimes of passion, restored haphazard rape, multiplied
acts of indecent exposure, authentic sources of poetry"] (MSM, 50).
He has long since moved beyond such open and openly violent ir-
reverence. Nonetheless, openness has its virtues. What is explicit
here is implicit in the tension of the work to follow. Passionate killing, rape, and indecent exposure are among the authentic sources of
poetry, says Char. The violence of this conception, and the poet's
evident wish to shock by articulating it, may be attenuated with age.
The pull toward homicide and exhibitionism may go underground.
But they do not go away. We have already seen the ubiquity of
violence in Char's poetry. We may add here that the ellipsis and
hermeticism of his work are linked to that violence and exist, to
some extent, in response to the force of his desire for exposure—as
it clashes with a native "pudeur" and a deep conviction that art
must, to do its work, transcend the individual, must show and
shelter worlds beyond him which too great an interest in self-
exposition might block out. During the war he wrote: "J'écris
brièvement. Je ne puis guère *m'absenter* longtemps. S'étaler con-
duirait à l'obsession. L'adoration des bergers n'est plus utile à la
planète" ["I write briefly. I can scarcely *absent myself* for long.
Spreading oneself out would lead to obsession. The adoration of the
shepherds is no longer useful to the planet"] (FM, 94; Char's italics).
On one level we may understand this to mean that his Resistance
duties call him away from the page. But, on another level, is it not
the exigencies of poetry itself that call him away from a lengthy
dwelling on his own person? To spread oneself out—literally, to
display oneself—would lead to obsession. Ellipsis and brevity are
called for on the page, as urgently as action is called for in the world.
Long, slow, passive adoration no longer serves any purpose.

However, as Char says in "Pour renouer," he must measure his
ellipsis carefully, lest what he shows seem less than what he hides.

"Le poète est la genèse d'un être qui projette et d'un être qui retient. A l'amant il emprunte le vide, à la bien-aimée, la lumière. Ce couple formel, cette double sentinelle lui donnent pathétiquement sa voix" ["The poet is the genesis of a being who projects and a being who holds back. From the lover he borrows emptiness, from the beloved, light. This formal couple, this double sentinel, gives him, touchingly, his voice"] (FM, 77). But then the question comes, to whom does the voice address itself in the third stanza of "Pour renouer," who is the "tu" in this poem? On one level, we feel it to be the reader; on another, the poem itself, which mediates between the two and which, in the following stanza, is seen to be a "wayside altar of darkness on [the poet's] too-exposed face."

In an extraordinarily layered image, the text stands not only between the poet and his reader, allowing the former to "show," "give," and "hide" (his poetic vision, his self) in relation to others, but it also stands between the poet and himself: it would seem to rest on his face, and between this altar of obscurity and his own vulnerability have slipped his splendor and his suffering. Slipped between, and stayed? Or slipped through like the snake, the meteor, to leave behind them shimmering absence, traces only of what was there but is gone: the poet's presence, whole (". . .for I have slipped / Your grasp, I have eluded"⁴)? The image recalls much of Char's bestiary, as it flees out of sight into shadow. And it recalls the following lines from another text which deals directly with the poet in relation to his poetry, "A***" ["To ***"]:

> Fermée comme un volet de buis
> Une extrême chance compacte
> Est notre chaîne de montagnes,
> Notre comprimante splendeur.
>
> Je dis chance, ô ma martelée;
> Chacun de nous peut recevoir
> La part de mystère de l'autre
> Sans en répandre le secret;
> Et la douleur qui vient d'ailleurs
> Trouve enfin sa séparation
> Dans la chair de notre unité,
> Trouve enfin sa route solaire
> Au centre de notre nuée
> Qu'elle déchire et recommence. . . .
>
> [RBS, 176]

Closed like a boxwood shutter,
Compressed to its limit, chance
Is our range of mountains,
Our constricting splendor.

I say chance, my hammered-out love;
Each of us can contain
The other's share of mystery
Without releasing the secret,
And the pain which comes from outside
Finds its separation at last
In the flesh of our unity,
At last finds its solar road
In the center of our cloud
It rends and begins again. . . .

Patricia Terry

Here, the woman poetry and her "désirant," the poet who
desires her (CB, 71), are enclosed together within the compressed
splendor of the poem. Each of them shares his or her mystery with
the other, but keeps it a secret, and exterior pain like a ray of sun
("ma splendeur et ma souffrance") periodically pierces through the
flesh of their unity ("se sont glissés entre les deux"), there to be
dissipated, tearing the lovers apart in the process and reconstituting
them, so that they are made new. Their cloud, their "nuée," contains a nakedness akin to the vulnerability of the poet's "face trop
offerte" in "Pour renouer," a nakedness which gives its name to
one of Char's major collections, *Le nu perdu* [*Nakedness Lost*], and to
the title poem of that collection, which reads in part: "Porteront
rameaux ceux dont l'endurance sait user la nuit noueuse qui précède
et suit l'éclair. . . .La rage des vents les maintient encore dévêtus.
Contre eux vole un duvet de nuit noire" ["They will bear palms,
whose endurance has learned to consume the gnarled night which
precedes and follows the lightning bolt. . . .The raging wind keeps
them still unclothed. Against them flies the down of darkest night"]
(NP, 31).

The poem clothes the poet ("Aux épines du torrent / Ma laine
maintient ma souffrance" ["Amidst the torrent's thorns / My wool
maintains my suffering"], he writes elsewhere [LM, 37]. The poem
in its rich complexity allows him to expose himself as much as he
dares: "Emerge autant que possible à ta propre surface. Que le ris-

que soit ta clarté. Comme un vieux rire. Dans une entière modestie"
["Rise to your own surface as much as possible. May risk be your
brightness. Like an old laugh. In total modesty."](RBS, 168). The
poem veils the poet's nakedness and his naked vision of a world he
wishes to exhibit and preserve and therefore must hide from the
reader, even as he shows it. For as we have said throughout this
essay, at every turning of this hunt, what is visible in Char's world
perishes, mysteries approached dissolve, seeing is equivalent to
touching—what cannot be touched without breakage or corrosion.
And in the last lines of "Pour renouer," it is a question of *seeing*:

> Jeter bas l'existence laidement accumulée et retrouver le
> regard qui l'aima assez à son début pour en étaler le fonde-
> ment. Ce qui me reste à vivre est dans cet assaut, dans ce
> frisson.

We have already quoted the poet's determination at the end of
the war to discard the "treasure" accumulated during the
Resistance, to cast aside his past, no matter how essential, so that he
can get back to his first way of looking, "dans une insatisfaction
nue, une connaissance à peine entrevue et une humilité question-
neuse" ["in naked dissatisfaction, knowledge scarcely glimpsed and
questioning humility"] (FM, 138). This is the way a poet must look,
this is true *voyance*; he must see as a child does, instantly, without
prior knowledge, unprotected, with wonder only and the desire to
share his vision of life's substructure—which is mystery. His eyes
must be unclouded, his words as bright and swift (elliptical) as
lightning so they can communicate how veiled and inviolable existence truly is. "The earth is essentially self-secluding," says
Heidegger. "To set forth the earth means to bring it into the Open
as the self-secluding."[5] "Pour renouer" sets forth the earth, reveals
it and its beauty and the poet who is their ally as essentially self-
secluding. The text is a veil Char places between us and the beauty
we are threatening. Mystery is the subject and the substance of this
poem.

It is a mystery threatened, but capable of being rehabilitated,
Char believes. And this belief contributes to the poet's own
mystery:

> Qui croit renouvelable l'énigme, la devient. Escaladant
> librement l'érosion béante, tantôt lumineux, tantôt obscur,
> savoir sans fonder sera sa loi. Loi qu'il observera mais qui

aura raison de lui; fondation dont il ne voudra pas mais qu'il
mettra en oeuvre.

On doit sans cesse en revenir à l'érosion. La douleur contre
la perfection. [NP, 130. Char's italics]

———————

Whoever believes the enigma renewable, becomes it. Now
luminous, now dim, freely scaling the yawning erosion, to
know without founding will be his law. A law he will observe
but which will get the better of him; a foundation he will want
none of, but which he will get under way.

One must ceaselessly come back to erosion. Pain against
perfection.

The poet, because he believes it "renewable," *becomes* the enigma.
"Tantôt lumineux, tantôt obscur" ("ce que je te montre" / "ce que
je te cache"), he slips in and out of our field of vision, knowing, but
refusing to found anything—systems, kingdoms, servitudes. Like
his comrade in arms, Rimbaud, "Il ne s'établit pas" ["He doesn't
establish himself"] (RBS, 131). His enemy is "l'érosion béante,"
which he scales like a fortress; and defeats, by means of poetry:

APRÈS

· ·
    La laideur! Ce contre quoi nous appelons n'est pas la
laideur opposable à la beauté, dont les arts et le désir effacent
et retracent continuellement la frontière. Laideur vivante,
beauté, toutes deux les énigmatiques, sont réellement inef-
fables. Celle qui nous occupe, c'est la laideur qui décompose
sa proie. Elle a surgi—plus délétère, croyons-nous, que par le
passé où on l'entrevit quelquefois—des flaques, et des
moisissures que le flot grossi des chimères, des cauchemars
comme des vraies conquêtes de notre siècle, a laissées en se
retirant.
    Alors, quel aliment?
    La liberté n'est pas ce qu'on nous montre sous ce nom.
Quand l'imagination, ni sotte, ni vile n'a, la nuit tombée,
qu'une parodie de fête devant elle, la liberté n'est pas de lui
jeter n'importe quoi pour tout infecter. La liberté protège le
silence, la parole et l'amour. Assombris, elle les ravive; elle
ne les macule pas. Et la révolte la ressuscite à l'aurore, si

longue soit celle-ci à s'accuser. La liberté, c'est de dire la vérité, avec des précautions terribles, sur la route où TOUT se trouve. [RBS, 53]

_____

AFTERWARDS

. . . .

Ugliness! What we are crying out against isn't the ugliness opposable to beauty, whose frontiers are constantly erased and redrawn by the arts and by desire. Living ugliness, beauty—both enigmatic—are truly ineffable. What concerns us is the ugliness that decomposes its prey. It has loomed up—more deadly than in the past, we think—from the puddles and the moldy spots left behind at the shrinkage of this century's swollen tide of myth and nightmare, along with its real triumphs.

Then what can nourish us?

Freedom is not what we are offered under that name. When, at nightfall, the imagination has before it the parody of a feast, it is not freedom to fling out just anything, thereby polluting the whole table. Freedom protects silence, speech, and love. When they grow clouded, it brightens them; it does not blemish them. And rebellion revives freedom at dawn, no matter how long that hour is in coming. Freedom consists in telling the truth, with extreme caution, on the road where EVERYTHING is found.

We think of the warbler in the reeds, whose song is pure freedom and who, singing in her frail invisibility, reestablishes the *site*, the transparent beauty and unity of the earth and the liberty of all those who dwell therein. The warbler *is* freedom. And so is the poet, for he speaks the truth, carefully, on the road where EVERYTHING is found. But if he is freedom, he is not free.

_____

Across the privileged space of the page there flees a Charian fiction whom the poet calls the "poet," an ink-and-paper creature who shares with the swift his elusiveness, who is as haunted as the melancholy hunter and as metaphorical as the meteor of August 13th. We know what a hunter does, what a meteor is. But what does the "poet" do? Who is he?

POURQUOI LA JOURNÉE VOLE

Le poète s'appuie, durant le temps de sa vie, à quelque arbre, ou mer, ou talus, ou nuage d'une certaine teinte, un moment, si la circonstance le veut. Il n'est pas soudé à l'égarement d'autrui. Son amour, son saisir, son bonheur ont leur equivalent dans tous les lieux où il n'est pas allé, où jamais il n'ira, chez les étrangers qu'il ne connaîtra pas. Lorsqu'on élève la voix devant lui, qu'on le presse d'accepter des égards qui retiennent, si l'on invoque à son propos les astres, il répond qu'il est du pays d'*à côté*, du ciel qui vient d'être englouti.

Le poète vivifie puis court au dénouement.

Au soir, malgré sur sa joue plusieurs fossettes d'apprenti, c'est un passant courtois qui brusque les adieux pour être là quand le pain sort du four. [LPA, 141. Char's italics]

WHY THE DAY FLIES

During his lifetime the poet leans against some tree or sea or slope or cloud of a certain color, for a moment, if circumstance permits. He is not welded to other people's aberrations. His love, his captivation, his happiness have equivalents in all the places he has never been, will never go, in strangers he will never meet. When voices are raised before him, offering honors which would bind, if someone speaking of him invokes the stars, he answers that he's from the *next* country, from the sky just now engulfed.

The poet quickens, then races to the outcome.

In the evening, though dimpled like an apprentice, he is a courteous passerby who cuts his farewells short to be there when the bread comes out of the oven.

This courtly passerby, the poet, makes the day fly. But no faster than he. What allows him to quicken—to vivify—as he passes is the fact of his passage. He is not "soldered" ("soudé) to the general bewilderment, he is separate. He refuses honors that would bind. Fixed stars are of no interest to him. Meteoric, his appearance as abrupt and discontinuous as the lightning's, his presence as marginal as the snake's—who, like him, is in a rush to get away—the poet pauses (for a moment only and only under favorable circumstances) to lean against a tree, or a cloud, if the color pleases him, but he does not settle down. "S'il te faut repartir," begins another of Char's poems, "prends appui contre une maison sèche" ["If you have to leave again, lean against a dry house"] (NP, 115). The poet always starts out anew, the dry house that supports him momentarily: the poem. He remains upright (*debout*), if slightly tilted, even when he stops. But mostly he moves, quickening, attracted by what quickens, not by long adieux but by things newly made, the bread as it leaves the oven—

> Je me redis, Beauté,
> Ce que je sais déjà,
> Beauté mâchurée
> D'excréments, de brisures,
> Tu es mon amoureuse,
> Je suis ton désirant.
> Le pain que nous cuisons
> Dans les nuits avenantes,
> Tel un vieux roi s'avance
> En ouvrant ses deux bras. . . .
>
> [CB, 71]

> I tell myself again, Beauty,
> What I already know,
> Beauty broken,
> Smudged with excrement,
> You are my lover,
> I am your pursuer.
> The bread we bake
> In the comely night
> Like an old king coming forward
> His arms open wide. . . . .

"A une rose je me lie" ["I bind myself to a rose"], Char writes in "Les compagnons dans le jardin" ("Companions in the Garden," LPA, 151). His only tie is to that which cannot secure him, for it is ephemeral. He can embrace the evanescent, but he flees stability, accumulation, *comfort*, for these are incompatible with art: "Confort est crime, m'a dit la source en son rocher" ["Comfort is crime, I was told by the spring in its rock"] (RBS, 181). Only traces subsist, when he has gone.

The poet is an exile, perpetually marginal. A stranger to those around him, "il vient du pays d'à côte, du ciel qui vient d'être englouti." Even when he travels he is on the fringe, for he takes "La route par les sentiers" ["The Road by the Paths"]:

Les sentiers, les entailles qui longent invisiblement la
route, sont notre unique route, à nous qui parlons pour vivre,
qui dormons, sans nous engourdir, sur le côté. [LPA, 179]

The paths, the grooves that run invisibly along the side of the road, are the only road for us—who speak in order to live, who sleep, without growing sluggish, on our side.

Of course he sleeps on his side. It is his own margin. And this position, like leaning against a tree instead of sitting down, only half commits him. He can take off again at any moment like the lightning. Whether moving, then, or temporarily immobile, the poet keeps to edges, he is apart. Necessarily. "Créer: s'exclure" ["To create: to exclude oneself"] (RBS, 152).

Nor does he simply separate himself from society. Char writes: "Il faut s'établir à l'extérieur de soi, au bord des larmes et dans l'orbite des famines, si nous voulons que quelque chose hors du commun se produise, qui n'était que pour nous" ["We must take up our abode outside ourselves, at the edge of tears and in the orbit of famines, if we want something out of the ordinary to come into existence, which was for us alone"] (LPA, 193). The corollary to the poet's stepping away from common presence into invisibility is his stepping out of himself, transcending his "sottise particulière" ["particular foolishness"] (NT, 71), to create something larger, universal, "le dessein de la poésie étant de nous rendre souverain en nous impersonnalisant. . ." ["poetry's purpose being to make us supreme by impersonalizing us"] (LPA, 116). He is his own prey, but only by leaving his "fragile house" can he hope to capture himself: "Le chasseur de soi fuit sa maison fragile: / Son gibier le suit n'ayant plus peur" ["The self-hunter flees his fragile house: / His game follows him, no longer afraid"] (FM, 171).

Here, then, are two perpetually reaffirmed absences—from society and from self—forced on the poet by his art. They are not the only ones. Absence characterizes the poet's most intimate relationship, his relationship with his reader, a stranger "qu'il ne connaîtra pas," to whom he, the poet, is "mortellement visible" in his text. Char writes, in "Partage formel" ["The Formal Share"]: "Au seuil de la pesanteur, le poète comme l'araignée construit sa route dans le ciel. En partie caché à lui-même, il apparaît aux autres, dans les rayons de sa ruse inouïe, mortellement visible" ["At the threshold of gravity, the poet like the spider builds his road in the sky. Partly hidden from himself, he appears to others in the spokes of his extraordinary ruse, mortally visible"] (FM, 76). A spider spinning at the threshold of gravity, at the margin between earth and sky, climbing out of heaviness into transparency, the poet sheds his flesh for word, he builds a road up out of self—like the road he followed with Jeanne/Anoukis, up to "that end of self we call a summit," but made of gossamer, invisible. He cannot judge just how much he has exposed, just what is showing in his poem, for it hides him partially from himself, it blinds him, this sun-shaped web, the ruse designed to capture others, which holds him fatally visible in its rays. The poem is a trap which catches poet and reader ("Le poète recommande: 'Penchez-vous, penchez-vous davantage.'" ["The poet urges: 'Lean over, lean further over. . .'"] [FM, 78]), creating them both—there can be no poet, no reader if there is no poem—and mediating between them. But mediating between them in their necessary absence from one another. "Comment m'entendez-vous?" writes Char. "Je parle de si loin. . ." ["How can you hear me? I'm speaking from so far away. . ."] (FM, 109).

And there is still another separation that the poet acts out again and again and again: his separation from his poem, once it has been written. The very nature of his art is discontinuous, and indeed it is the discontinuity of poetry that helps to make it durable for Char, who says, "L'éclair me dure" ["The lightning lasts me"] (LPA, 146). But if it is true that each separate poem captures an instant and renders it eternal, this in no way makes the poet himself more secure. "Magicien de l'insécurité, le poète n'a que des satisfactions adoptives. Cendre toujours inachevée" ["A magician of insecurity, the poet has only adoptive satisfactions. Never-finished ash."] (FM, 66). When the last verse has been composed, another poem must be begun. The poet must start from scratch ("L'acte est vierge, même répété" ["The act is virgin, even if repeated"] [FM, 98]), from zero, without any guarantees. "Le poète ne retient pas ce qu'il découvre; l'ayant transcrit, le perd bientôt. En cela réside sa nouveauté, son infini et son péril" ["The poet does not hold onto what he discovers; having transcribed it, soon loses it. This makes him new, infinite, endangered"] (LPA, 147). The poet lets his poems go, just as he lets his lovers go. In poetry, as in love, he leaves. But he comes back:

> Tu es mon amour depuis tant d'années,
> Mon vertige devant tant d'attente,

Que rien ne peut vieillir, froidir;
Même ce qui attendait notre mort,
Ou lentement sut nous combattre,
Même ce qui nous est étranger,
Et mes éclipses et mes retours.

[RBS, 176]

You have been my love for so many years,
Vertiginous depths of my waiting,
That nothing can age or cool;
Even what lay in wait for our death,
Or slowly found out how to fight us,
Even the alien things,
And myself in eclipse and coming back.

Patricia Terry

Eclipse is followed by return, for if the poet finishes the individual poem he never finishes his poetry. In this sense, he is a meteor that never ceases burning—although he periodically becomes invisible—and never ceases moving on, a nomad spark forever dying in its fire.

Sometimes in this couple, poet/Poetry, it is the other partner who absents herself. Poetry is not uninterrupted, but rather "le jeu des berges arides" ["the play of arid riverbanks"] (FM, 101), and it abandons the poet at times, to his deepest anguish. Then, he has said, he sees the rose, but putrified, "disgusting." Then he is truly "homme de berges—creusement et inflammation—ne pouvant l'être toujours de torrent" ["a man of the riverbanks—digging and inflammation—unable always to be a man of the torrent"] (FM, 132). And only with the greatest patience, at the end of vertiginous waiting and desire, is he able, as he has said, to "reconstitute the rose" by writing it again.[6] These arid desert times he calls the compost heap, the humus, out of which his poems grow.

"La beauté naît du dialogue, de la rupture du silence et du regain de ce silence" ["Beauty is born of dialogue, of the breaking of silence and the renewal of that silence"] (FM, 188).

Severance and union, silence and speech, sterility and fertility—the poet fluctuates between them, ever mobile, flamelike. Each time he writes, he flashes forward, risking himself in the encounter that will produce his poem: "Impose ta chance, serre ton

bonheur et va vers ton risque. A te regarder, *ils* s'habitueront"
["Impose your luck, embrace your happiness, and go toward your
risk. Watching you, *they* will adapt"] (LM, 75; Char's italics). Then
he disappears, forward. The poet does not go back, he goes on.
Sometimes explosively, as in "Le mortel partenaire," sometimes
with less violence, though with scarcely less speed, as in "Pourquoi
la journée vole." Spasms. And this spasmodic movement, the very
pulse of poetry (as it is the very pulse of love), is given form, personified within his work not only by the lightning bolt and by such
creatures as the swift, the snake, and the goldfinch, but also by a
series of human creatures: in addition to Char's fictive "poet," the
fragrant gatherer of mimosas, the "Transparents" ["Transparent
Ones"]—those "vagabonds luni-solaires" ["luni-solar vagabonds"]
who are blood brothers to the poet in their mobility and marginality,
and also in their rhymed speech (LM, 28–35), the seductive
wanderer in "Compagnie de l'écolière" [The School Girl's Company"], the narrator of "La compagne du vannier." All of these
highly mobile beings appear and disappear, causing a disturbance in
the fixed surroundings they pass through. They leave the people
whose paths they cross, and the reader is among these, changed. All
of them experience—and communicate—"l'électricité du voyage"
["the electricity of the voyage"] (FM, 30), which is one way to
describe writing, and reading. Char says, "Nous sommes des
passants *appliqués* à passer, donc à jeter le trouble, à infliger notre
chaleur, à dire notre exubérance. Voilà pourquoi nous sommes in-
tempestifs et insolites!" ["We are passersby who *apply ourselves* to
passing—to causing trouble, inflicting our warmth, articulating our
exuberance. That is why we are unseasonable and rare!"] (LM, 80;
his italics). These passersby are studious, insistent. They inflict
their warmth, they *mark* us, and the page, consciously striving to
disrupt by means of their own intense mobility. And among the
many rapid travelers in Char's work who arrive just long enough to
take their leave, transforming us, appears Arthur Rimbaud.

He is an exemplary figure in the Charian universe, a great poet,
violent and visionary, who left. He actually lived out the departure
Char repeatedly attributes to his metaphorical "poète." But this
departure he accomplished in his poetry first (which makes us think
again of Proust):

> Rimbaud s'évadant situe indifféremment son âge d'or
> dans le passé et dans le futur. Il ne s'établit pas. Il ne fait
> surgir un autre temps, sur le mode de la nostalgie ou celui du

désir, que pour l'abattre aussitôt et revenir dans le présent, cette cible au *centre* toujours affamé de projectiles, ce port naturel de tous les départs. Mais de l'en deçà à l'au delà, la crispation est extraordinaire. Rimbaud nous en fournit la relation. Dans le mouvement d'une dialectique ultra-rapide, mais si parfaite qu'elle n'engendre pas un *affolement,* mais un tourbillon ajusté et précis qui emporte toute chose avec lui, insérant dans un devenir sa charge de temps pur, il nous entraîne, il nous soumet, consentants.

Chez Rimbaud, la *diction* précède d'un adieu la *contradiction*. Sa découverte, sa date incendiaire, c'est la rapidité. L'empressement de sa parole, son étendue épousent et couvrent une surface que le verbe jusqu'à lui n'avait jamais atteinte ni occupée. En poésie, on n'habite que le lieu que l'on quitte, on ne crée que l'oeuvre dont on se détache, on n'obtient la durée qu'en detruisant le temps. Mais tout ce qu'on obtient par rupture, détachement et négation, on ne l'obtient que pour autrui. La prison se referme aussitôt sur l'évadé. Le donneur de liberté n'est libre que dans les autres. Le poète ne jouit que de la liberté des autres. [RBS, 131–132. Char's italics]

Escaping us, Rimbaud situates his golden age indifferently in the past and in the future. He does not establish himself. He only evokes another time, on a note of nostalgia or desire, to demolish it immediately, returning to the present, that target whose *center* always craves projectiles, that natural port of all departures. But from this side to that side what an extraordinary contraction. Rimbaud connects for us. In the movement of an ultra-rapid dialectic, so perfect it does not engender panic—an ordered and precise whirlwind which carries everything along with it, inserting into flux its charge of pure time—he captures us, he conquers us, consenting.

In Rimbaud's work, *diction* precedes *contradiction* with a goodbye. His discovery, his incendiary date, is speed. The haste of his speech, his scope, marry and cover a surface which the word before him had never attained nor occupied. In poetry you only dwell in the place you leave, you only create the work from which you separate, you obtain duration only by destroying time. But whatever is achieved by breakage, detachment, and negation is achieved only for others. The prison immediately closes again on the escaped prisoner. The freedom-giver is only free in others. The poet enjoys only the freedom of others.

Rimbaud escapes us within his work. He will not be fixed, he moves continuously back and forth in time and ends inevitably in the present, a target and a point of departure (both charged terms for Char). The question is how does Rimbaud move so far, how does he get from here to there and take us with him, "insérant dans un devenir sa charge de temps pur"? Char's response—Rimbaud's "découverte"—is *rapidity*. He must be as quick as lightning to cover so much ground; and speed ensures his getaway. *Il dessèche le tonnerre.* Before the reader can have second thoughts, he is gone: "Chez Rimbaud, la *diction* précède d'un adieu la *contradiction.*" One of the necessary components of his ultra-rapid dialectic is ellipsis. He disappears, leaves things out, does not dwell on anything, does not explain along the way. He simply goes. ("Aller me suffit.") He is elliptical and faster than the eye can see, and with the onrush of his words and his ensuing silence, he brings us to submission—we are his—consenting.

This also happens in the poetry of René Char, whose tone is a clenched serenity, whose words strike like the lightning to transfix the reader, while the poet's splendor and his suffering slip through. He has written recently:

> A l'horizon de l'écriture: l'incertitude, et la poussée d'une énergie gagnante. Le dardillon autour duquel va s'enrouler la concrète nébuleuse se précise. Une bouche pourra bientôt proférer. Quoi? Rien de moins dessiné qu'un mot venu de l'écart et du lointain, qui ne devra son salut qu'à la vélocité de sa course. [CB, 79]

> ———

> On the horizon of writing: uncertainty, and the thrust of a growing energy. The barb around which the concrete nebula will wind itself grows more precise. Soon a mouth will be able to proffer it. What? There is nothing less clearly delineated than a word, born of separation and distance, which owes its salvation only to the velocity of its voyage.

Speed and ellipsis. The word like a bullet, a dart, pointed. Around it forms the poem, a nebula, a meteor, or meteorite, a knot of iron, "Le noeud noir" ["Black Knot"] (CB, 71), that survives the burning, rapid fall, or becomes it altogether. In poems like "Le martinet," "Congé au vent," "Réception d'Orion," Char's language is so beautiful and so compact ("une extrême chance compacte") that these texts strike us, glimmering, with what has not been said—"Mais peut-être notre coeur n'est-il formé que de la réponse qui n'est point donnée?" ["But isn't our heart perhaps formed only by the answer which is never given?"] (LPA, 119)—and we consent, illuminated.

L'ARBRE FRAPPÉ

(I)
La foudre spacieuse et le feu du baiser
Charmeront mon tombeau par l'orage dressé.

(II)
Enlevé par l'oiseau à l'éparse douleur,
Et laissé aux forêts pour un travail d'amour.

[LPA, 157]

STRICKEN TREE

(I)
The spacious lightning and the fire of a kiss
Will charm my tomb set up by the storm.

(II)
Carried off by the bird of scattered pain,
And left to the forests for a work of love.

Writer, reader struck. The tree afire. The bird-poet seeds the page, so that the poem may do its work. *Un travail d'amour.*

The "poet" is as swift and mobile as his imagery, as the other fictions living in his text. He never establishes himself, but though he leaves, he is not free. Char tells us in his essay on Rimbaud that after every poem—every poem being an escape—the prison door slams to, again. For if it is so that "in poetry you only dwell in the place you leave, you only create the work from which you separate, you obtain duration only by destroying time," it is equally true that the poet's repeated acts of severance leave him repeatedly with empty hands: "Whatever is achieved by breakage, detachment, and negation is achieved only for others." Both the poet and his melancholy hunter watch as everything they touch goes up in smoke. "The freedom-giver is only free in others. The poet enjoys only the freedom of others." He shares with the warbler in the reeds and with *la détenue* ["the detained woman"] in "La vérité vous rendra libres" ["Truth Shall Make You Free"] a liberating (for others) bondage. He is in some sense locked into his own freedom and his own lucidity ("La lucidité est la blessure la plus rapprochée du soleil" ["Lucidity is the wound closest to the sun."] [FM, 130]). He is forever on the road. Like the meteor, "Sa marche ne connaît qu'un terme: la mort" ["His going knows only one end: death."] (RBS, 132).

> Le poète, on le sait, mêle le manque et l'excès, le but et le passé. D'où l'insolvabilité de son poème. Il est dans la malédiction, c'est-à-dire qu'il assume de perpétuels et renaissants périls, autant qu'il refuse, les yeux ouverts, ce que d'autres acceptent, les yeux fermés: le profit d'être poète. Il ne saurait exister de poète sans appréhension pas plus qu'il n'existe de poèmes sans provocation. Le poète passe par tous les degrés solitaires d'une gloire collective dont il est, de bonne guerre, exclu. C'est la condition pour sentir et dire juste. [RBS, 35–36]

> It is well known that the poet mixes deficiency and excess, the target and the past. Whence the insolvency of his poem. He is under a curse, in that he takes on perpetual and perpetually renewed dangers, just as he refuses, open-eyed, what others close their eyes to accept: the profit of being a poet. There could not exist a poet without apprehension, no more than poems could exist without provocation. The poet passes through all the solitary degrees of a collective glory from which he is, quite fairly, excluded. This is the necessary condition for feeling and speaking correctly.

The poet's separateness and solitude are the conditions of his art. "Je suis l'exclu et le comblé" ["I am the excluded one, and the fulfilled"], writes Char (FM, 46). And again, "Créer: s'exclure. Quel créateur ne meurt pas désespéré? Mais est-on désespéré si l'on est déchiré? Peut-être pas" ["To create: to exclude oneself. What creator does not die in despair? But does one despair if one is torn apart? Perhaps not"] (RBS, 152). Let us look at "Montagne déchirée":

MONTAGNE DÉCHIRÉE
Oh! la toujours plus rase solitude
Des larmes qui montent aux cimes.

Quand se déclare la débâcle
Et qu'un vieil aigle sans pouvoir
Voit revenir son assurance,
Le bonheur s'élance à son tour,
A flanc d'abîme les rattrape.

Chasseur rival, tu n'as rien appris,
Toi qui sans hâte me dépasses
Dans la mort que je contredis.

Le Rébanqué, Lagnes, 29 August 1949

[LM, 51]

TORN MOUNTAIN

Oh! ever barer solitude
Of the tears rising to the peaks.

When the collapse arrives
And an old eagle without power
Sees his confidence come back,
Happiness in its turn shoots forth,
Catching them at the verge of the abyss.

Rival hunter, you've learned nothing,
You who without haste move ahead
Into death that I contradict.
Jonathan Griffin

We have come full circle, back to birds. But this is no warbler. This old eagle—"un Sisyphe oiseau" ["a Sisyphus bird"] (RBS, 66)—rivals the poet at the hunt, and slowly outstrips him in his solitary, ever-repeated flight to the top of the torn mountain.

The eagle in Char's poetry is usually equated with the artist, often the visual artist. Thus, the poet calls Giacometti "le vieil aigle despote" ["the old despotic eagle"] (NP, 32), and writes of Braque:

> Aigle celui que sa plume longue, son aile froide, mènent le plus haut, emportent au plus loin. Hôte du bois pauvre et de la caillasse, roitelet celui que le serpent guette tant il vole bas et son sang est chaud. Les deux ont demeure chez mon ami. [RBS, 66]

> Eagle, he whose long feather and cold wing take him the highest, carry him the furthest away. Guest of meager wood

and pebbles, wren, he whom the serpent watches for, so low
does he fly, so warm his blood. These two reside in my
friend.

Braque is both wren and eagle, vulnerable and out of sight. He flies
so low he makes the serpent salivate, but then too his long cold
wings take him to the upper air. And most assuredly this may be
said of Char.

In "Montagne déchirée" the poet and the eagle parallel each
other: both climb toward the summit, the "end of self," the end too
of clustered humanity, communal birds, and thick-grown plants, up
into ellipsis and stripped vision, toward "le nu perdu," sheer rock
and ice, and barest solitude. Like the mountain on which they meet
for an instant, which is melting now, they are both torn apart by the
immense effort to rise, to rise out of themselves, and by the risks involved. For at the end of winter, of frozen immobility, it is not until
he has taken off, chanced flying—or falling—that the eagle (poet)
knows he can do it. Nor does he really have a choice:

> Nous ne pouvons vivre que dans l'entrouvert, exactement
> sur la ligne hermétique de partage de l'ombre et de la
> lumière. Mais nous sommes irrésistiblement jetés en avant.
> Toute notre personne prête aide et vertige à cette poussée.
> [LPA, 196]

> We can only live in the half-open, precisely on the
> hermetic line separating shadow and light. But we are ir-
> resistibly thrown forward. Our whole person lends force and
> vertigo to this thrust.

Thrust forward into flight, the solitary eagle feels his confidence
rejoin him and the two of them, in turn, are caught by "le bonheur."
Then he is rising, flying at the edge of the abyss, a majestic bird of
prey, marginal, alone and joyous, contradicting death as he confronts it. He has learned nothing, in the sense that he repeats this
flight that passes understanding again and again and again, and
toward a summit that seems ever higher—and ever more splendid,
once achieved:

> Je dis chance comme je le sens.
> Tu as élevé le sommet
> Que devra franchir mon attente
> Quand demain disparaîtra.
> [RBS, 176]

I say chance as it seems to me.
You have lifted up the summit
My waiting will have to cross
When tomorrow disappears.

Patricia Terry

Poetry is flight—forward—into extreme solitude, deep peril, up to vertiginous heights. Lit up by chance, poetry is hunting. The eagle-poet's flight in search of truth and beauty vanquishes death, and somewhere in the middle air, suspended, within sight of the chasm, his anguish is extinguished by his joy. Char writes, "La crainte, l'ironie, l'angoisse que vous ressentez en présence du poète qui porte le poème sur toute sa personne, ne vous méprenez pas, c'est du pur bonheur" ["The fear, the irony, the anguish you feel in the presence of the poet who wears his poem all over him—make no mistake, that is pure happiness"] (RBS, 171). Such is *la condition poétique*.

CONCLUSION

Le réel quelquefois désaltère l'espérance.
C'est pourquoi, contre toute attente,
l'espérance survit. [LPA, 153]

Sometimes what is real fulfills our hopes.
This is why, against all odds, hope survives.

Here is the poet in an exultant mood:

SEUIL

Quand s'ébranla le barrage de l'homme aspiré par la faille
géante de l'abandon du divin, des mots dans le lointain, des
mots qui ne voulaient pas se perdre, tentèrent de résister à
l'exorbitante poussée. Là se décida la dynastie de leur sens.

J'ai couru jusqu'à l'issue de cette nuit diluvienne. Planté
dans le flageolant petit jour, ma ceinture pleine de saisons, je
vous attends, ô mes amis qui allez venir. Déjà je vous devine
derrière la noirceur de l'horizon. Mon âtre ne tarit pas de
voeux pour vos maisons. Et mon bâton de cyprès rit de tout
son coeur pour vous. [FM, 181]

_____

THRESHOLD

When the dam, which man is, shifted—breathed in by that
giant crack, the abandonment of the divine—words in the
distance, words that were refusing to be lost, tried to resist
the exorbitant thrust. There the dynasty of their meaning was
decided.

I have run to the outcome of this diluvian night. Taking
my stand in the trembling dawn, with my belt full of seasons,
I am waiting for you, my friends who will come. Already I
divine you behind the black of the horizon. My hearth's good
wishes for your homes never dry up. And my cypress walking
stick laughs with its whole heart for you.

Jonathan Griffin

Our dam has broken in the sudden absence of the gods, and abruptly alone and vulnerable, our very words are about to perish, though they attempt resistance. Language is drowning, all sense, all possibility of communication swept before the flood, meanings no longer rooted as they were, but torn loose now and going under.

The poet, however, is a runner and a pessimist. We have seen that he perpetually assumes a state of risk, does not establish himself, just tentatively leans against a dry house, poised on the margin between present and future, at the threshold of gravity. Thus he is ready, when the giant fault gapes suddenly in "Seuil," to spring along it, along the line uniting light and fear, to get ahead of death, outdistancing the fatal waters, running through the vast diluvial night to found a dynasty, "fondation dont il ne voudra pas mais qu'il mettra en oeuvre" ["a foundation he will want none of, but which he will get under way"], thereby saving language. Former meanings may have been uprooted, but the poet himself is *planted* in the dawn, his belt full of seasons, full of ongoing life. In the trembling first light, he awaits us, his future readers, and he awaits the words that will arrive soon. He guesses at their presence within the prenatal darkness; his hearth overflows with good wishes for their houses, the future poems they will live in, and his walking stick laughs joyously at their advent.

Having gotten this far in our hunt, we recognize the many themes and images in Char's "Seuil" that we have encountered before. We meet once again the marginal, mobile poet, here as elsewhere far ahead of us and "far ahead of his life," an eagle already in the future, elusive as the swift or the Charian lightning bolt, solitary, yet fundamentally attached to the human community, whose lines of communication he is able to keep open precisely because of his marginality. We recognize the deeply felt loss of the divine and the violent consequences of that loss, and see again how Char relocates the sacred in the human creature and his world—his walking stick, his hearth, his belt, which suddenly take on the size of myth. We are reminded of René Girard's "monstrous double," that marginal being whose sacrificial death and subsequent apotheosis *found* society in *La violence et le sacré*. This is akin to what Char's poet does in "Seuil," struggling once again, as he does in so many other Charian texts, to counteract the wreckage of man's world—though this poem's flood is metaphorical, whereas elsewhere (*Le Soleil des eaux*, "Ruine d'Albion") the earth's destruction is quite literal.

The hour of "Seuil" is Charian: dawn, but a dawn born of Night, its blackness still brimming the horizon, beyond which death comes rising on the waters, just as does rebirth. We recognize that poetry is mortal combat, in other poems against a single opponent, here against a floodtide of destruction—nor are we strangers to that tide, having seen it recede from the text entitled "Après" to leave behind it that "ugliness which decomposes its prey," to which the poet opposed his own definition of freedom as our only possible means of salvation: "Freedom consists in telling the truth, with extreme caution, on the road where EVERYTHING is found." Freedom is synonymous with truest speech, which is precisely what the runner-poet in "Seuil" has salvaged. Thus, we recognize in him another Charian freedom giver, who ensures that celebration will be possible after catastrophe, for with his words he will create—has in the course of his brief text already created—the *site*. He stands on its threshold, waiting for us to join him.

We recognize too in this poem the Charian voice, at one and the same time transparent (no abstruse words to startle us) and complex (but what startling combinations of words), by turns distant—biblical, mythic—and familiar.

The ground covered between the first and second stanzas is immense and is reflected by a modulation in the poet's speech: its tone, its vocabulary, its images. In the course of the text we progress from the apocalyptic cracking of the dam and the ensuing biblical flood to a walking stick that laughs. Char evokes the apocalypse in language that is abstract, cosmic in dimension, distant in tone, giving us the poem's central metaphor in a vocabulary grand enough for the mouths of the gods, were they not in fact gone: "le barrage de l'homme," "la faille géante de l'abandon du divin," "l'exorbitante poussée," "la dynastie de leur sens," each of these phrases punctuated by the curt, incontrovertible death knell of the *passé simple*. Doom.

But with the short first sentence of the second stanza—indeed, with its first word—we move out of the general into the particular. The poet has outrun the diluvial night, and he will describe himself, to give us hope and to urge forward the words he has gotten so far ahead of. His speech becomes specific, personal, familiar—he directly addresses those he is awaiting—and in a striking series of displacements and metonymies he does away with doom, to offer joy. It is the daybreak, not he, whose legs are trembling with fatigue ("flageolant"); he himself is planted in the dawn, like a tree or a saxifrage. The poet is a man of unilateral stability. His belt filled with seasons makes of him an Orion figure—years before *Aromates chasseurs*—a constellation,[1] joining earth and sky, perched on the horizon, beyond which he senses future presences ("A l'horizon de l'écriture: l'incertitude, et la poussée d'une énergie gagnante" ["On the horizon of writing: uncertainty, and the thrust of a growing energy"]. All his verbs are suddenly in the present tense, even when they speak of past events ("j'ai couru"—not "je courus"),[2] even when they evoke future ones ("mes amis qui allez venir"—not "mes amis qui viendrez"). He is planted in the present, in the whiteness of his page, whose threshold will be crossed by words as they move out of blackness into the future poems that will house them, into this very poem as it comes into being.

A poem whose last lines, in their particularity, accomplish that salvaging of language—in its particularity—which is the subject of "Seuil." Char's movement at a linguistic level from the general to the specific parallels and embodies his movement at a thematic level from catastrophe to celebration, from apocalypse to resurrection. His hearth, he says, overflows with good wishes, will not dry up—the metonymy less striking, in the context of this poem, than the verb, which turns his hearth, normally the locus of fire, into a spring, a fountain, contained but abundant, in contrast to the death-dealing waters now let loose by fickle gods. (We think of Anoukis the Clasper, missing here.) And then the poem's last image, another metonymy, this one complicated and enriched by an additional metaphor: "my cypress walking stick laughs with its whole heart for you." A stick cannot laugh, has no heart, except in "Seuil." And this irreverent, last, joyous image causes us to marvel at what language can accomplish, and to join the poet in rejoicing at his gift.

––––––––––

His gift to us, his welcoming gesture comes at the end of a Heraclitean poem, not the first we have seen, wherein initial violence, flux, conflict lead to renewal. In another water text, "Le requin et la mouette" ["The Shark and the Seagull"], the poet writes: "O Vous, arc-en-ciel de ce rivage polisseur, approchez le navire de son espérance. Faites que toute fin supposée soit une neuve innocence, un fiévreux en-avant pour ceux qui trébuchent dans la matinale lourdeur" ["O You, rainbow of this smoothing shore, draw the ship close in to her hope. Make every imagined ending a new innocence, a feverish onward! for those who stumble in the heaviness of morning"] (FM, 190). Supposed endings are in fact rebirths for Char, new steps into a future not yet touched upon.

In the pages of this essay we have seen that despite its violence and pessimism and the constant presence of death, Char's poetry is vibrant with hope, exalting as it does the natural world and the ephemeral, accursed but self-transcendent human creature, and exalting that most wondrous of man's products, our rampart of twigs, Art. The poet talks about it, other people's and his own, throughout his work. He addresses text after text to Poetry, to the question of poetry, attempting to define it, attempting to define the poem, the poet. In this, he is a man of his time, a destitute time. "It is a necessary part of the poet's nature," writes Heidegger, "that before he can be truly a poet in such an age, the time's destitution must have made the whole being and vocation of the poet a poetic question for him. Hence 'poets in a destitute time' must especially gather in poetry the nature of poetry."[3]

Thus the last lines of "Le requin et la mouette," quoted above, clearly apply to the making of poems, to the vocation of poetry, which, as Char conceives of it, is marked by spasms, each poem an electrifying encounter followed by relinquishment. But then, this may be said of all the major adventures in the Charian universe—love, hunting, warfare, as well as poetry. In each of these, the privileged instant occurs, after long waiting, the Charian encounter, lightning-like, elusive, illuminating, dangerous. All of the creatures in this poet's universe, which is governed by the dialectic of desire, participate in what Char has called "une guérilla sans reproche." His birds and beasts, his lovely elusive women, his melancholy hunter, his meteors, all flash in and out of hiding, in and out of sight, as does the poet himself within his poetry, whose form is fragmentary, elliptical, a series of flashes, bullets, lightning bolts, whose language is as elusive as the snake, dwelling among us but invisibly. Char's language strikes us as both *hermétique* and *engagé*, transparent and yet shadowed often in a "verte obscurité" (CB, 73), exposing him and at the same time veiling him and his vision of the world and of life's mystery.

We have read "Pour renouer," in which he himself writes: "Tu es reposoir d'obscurité sur ma face trop offerte, poème" ["You are, poem, a wayside altar of darkness on my too-exposed face"]. The poem a shadowy altar, offering him to us, but in darkness. The poet's shadows act to protect him, for he is vulnerable in his necessary exposure and separateness—necessary, as expressed in "Seuil," if he is to do his work. And his shadows enhance, with distance and mystery, his art. But they are rent periodically, as is the cloud in "A***," by shafts of sunlight, flashes of illumination:

"Les ténèbres que tu t'infuses sont régies par la luxure de ton ascendant solaire" ["The darkness in which you steep yourself is subject to the lust of your solar ascendant"] (FM, 198). So that, as we suggested at the beginning of this essay, all of Char's work seems lit from within by the tension between concealment and revelation, distance and proximity, the visible and the invisible, his eclipse and his return, and the eclipse and the return of Poetry. He writes:

La poésie a un arrière-pays dont seule la clôture est sombre.
Nul pavillon ne flotte longtemps sur cette banquise qui, au gré de son caprice, se donne à nous et se reprend. Mais elle indique à nos yeux l'éclair et ses ressources vierges. [SP, 28]

_____

Poetry has a back country whose enclosure alone is dark.
No one's colors float for long on this ice floe which capriciously surrenders herself to us, then withdraws. But she opens our eyes to the lightning bolt and to the lightning's virgin resources.

The writing, the reading of René Char: electrifying encounters—followed by relinquishment—which like the lightning illuminate us and tear us apart, and, like the lightning, last.

Georges Braque, illustration for *Le Soleil des eaux* by René Char, © by ADAGP, Paris 1981.

NOTES

INTRODUCTION

[1]William Butler Yeats, "The Circus Animals' Desertion," *The Collected Poems of W.B. Yeats* (New York: Macmillan, 1956), p. 336.

[2]Private conversation with Helen Vendler, July 15, 1979.

[3]For a somewhat more detailed biography of Char than that which appears here, see Dominique Fourcade's "Chronologie" in *Cahiers de l'Herne* (Paris, 1971), pp. 11–15. It is striking, and characteristically so, that even Fourcade's more extensive biography stops abruptly—at the poet's own wish—in 1946.

[4]According to Char, the three poets actually composed the poems in this volume together. "Really?" I said: "How did that work?" "It didn't," he said. (Private conversation, March 25, 1972.)

[5]See, among others, Georges Mounin, *La communication poétique précédé de Avez-vous lu Char?* (Paris: Gallimard, 1969); Mary Ann Caws, *The Presence of René Char* (Princeton: Princeton University Press, 1976); James Lawler, *René Char: The Myth and The Poem* (Princeton: Princeton University Press, 1978).

[6]Dominique Fourcade, "Essai d'introduction," *L'Herne* (Paris, 1971), p. 22.

[7]Marcel Proust, *The Past Recaptured*, trans. Andreas Mayor (New York: Vintage Books, 1971), p. 158.

[8]See Gabriel Bounoure, "Céreste et la Sorgue," *L'Arc* 22 (Summer, 1963), 25–32.

CHAPTER 1:

[1]Gérard Genette, *Figures III* (Paris: Editions du Seuil, 1972), p. 30.

[2]Maurice Blanchot, *L'Entretien infini* (Paris: Gallimard, 1969), p. 445.

[3]The term *maquis* comes from a certain kind of low-lying vegetation in the Mediterranean region which was used by Corsican bandits and French Resistance fighters for cover. By extension, a very Charian extension, the plant gave its name to the undercover fighters themselves.

[4]Jean Starobinski, "René Char et la définition du poème," *Liberté* X, 4 (1968), 22.

[5]Private conversation with Char, June 9, 1979.

[6]This Charian verse, like many Charian verses, recalls Heidegger and Hölderlin, as quoted by Heidegger. See Heidegger's "The Thinker as Poet," *Poetry, Language, Thought*, trans. Albert Hofstadter (New York: Harper & Row, 1971), p. 13.

CHAPTER 2:

[1]René Girard, *La violence et le sacré* (Paris: Grasset, 1972), p. 76.

[2]Private conversation with Char, March 25, 1972.

[3]Heidegger, "Thinker as Poet," p. 7.

[4]Girard, p. 36.

CHAPTER 3:

[1]Jean-Pierre Richard, "René Char," *Onze études sur la poésie moderne* (Paris: Editions du Seuil, 1964), p. 98.

[2]For a detailed and illuminating analysis of Char's swift see Serge Gaulupeau, "Le savoir du coeur dans la poésie de René Char," *L'Herne* (Paris, 1971), pp. 95–107.

[3]Maurice Blanchot, "René Char et la pensée du neutre," *L'Entretien infini* (Paris: Gallimard, 1969), pp. 439–450.

[4]See my article, "The Sexualized Poetic Universe of René Char," *Stanford French Review* II, 1 (Spring, 1978), pp. 51–60.
And for a fascinating essay on the sexualization of the natural world in myths relating to the blacksmith and the alchemist—both brothers to the poet in Char's universe—see Mircea Eliade, *Forgerons et alchimistes* (Paris: Flammarion, 1977).

[5]One notable exception is James Lawler's reading: "René Char's *Quatre Fascinants*," in *About French Poetry from Dada to Tel Quel: Text and Theory*, ed. Mary Ann Caws (Detroit: Wayne State University Press, 1974). But although Lawler's close textual analysis yields many rich linguistic and thematic insights, he does not address the question of eroticism, nor does he show the close interrelationship between the four sections of the poem that arises, in large part, from its erotic dimension.

[6]During my visit to Char in June 1977, we two were looking at an illustration of "Quatre fascinants" when I asked the poet, "Who is *La Minutieuse?*" Char put his finger on the lark, so small in the picture that she is only a point in the sky. After a moment, he moved his finger to the bull and said, "Et voilà le poète."

[7]In W. K. C. Guthrie's *A History of Greek Philosophy* (Cambridge: Cambridge University Press, 1962), I: p. 453.

[8]Lawler, *"Quatre Fascinants,"* p. 211.

[9]It was during my first visit to Char in March 1972 that we discussed this particular text. See my dissertation, *Eclairs: A Study of Invisibility and Violence in the Poetry of René Char* (Tufts University, 1973). In the course of the conversation he remarked, among other things, that "Le serpent" is a "poème féministe."
An alternate version of the first half of this poem appeared in *Cahiers du Sud* (No. 300 [1950]: 217), subsequently disappeared in favor of the version I am using, and has now reappeared in the recently published *Poems of René Char*, translated and annotated by Mary Ann Caws and Jonathan Griffin: "Prince des contresens, fais que mon amour / En exil analogue à ton banissement / Echappe au vieux Seigneur que je hais d'avoir pu / Après l'avoir troublé, en clair le décevoir." But these lines strike me as being more awkward and not much clearer than the version appearing in all other anthologies, and I have thus retained the latter.

CHAPTER 4:

[1]Starobinski, "Définition du poème," 28.

[2]Girard, p. 348.

³*Egyptian Mythology*, trans. Delano Ames (from *Mythologie Générale Larousse*) (New York: Prometheus Press, 1965), p. 108.

⁴Ibid., p. 108.

⁵Heidegger, "Thinker as Poet," p. 10.

⁶*Egyptian Mythology*, p. 106.

⁷See "The Origin of the Work of Art" in Heidegger's *Poetry, Language, Thought.*

⁸Private conversation with Char, March 25, 1972.

⁹Private conversation with Char, June 9, 1979.

¹⁰Starobinski, p. 24.

¹¹Georges Bataille, *L'érotisme* (Paris: Collection 10/18, 1975), p. 15.

¹²Maurice Blanchot, *La part du feu,* (Paris: Gallimard, 1949), p. 114.

¹³Roger Caillois, *L'homme et le sacré* (Paris: Gallimard, 1950), p. 19.

CHAPTER 5:

¹In between these two ("Le météore du 13 août" and Orion) there burns a third: "Tradition du météore," published in *Le nu perdu* in 1971. This text has been extensively analyzed by Piero Bigongiari in *L'Herne*, p. 67-70.

²Mounin, *Communication poétique*, p. 58.

³For a complete, if naive, account of my discussion with Char of this verse and others containing like imagery (e.g., "Il y a une sorte d'homme toujours en avance sur ses excréments"), see my dissertation, pp. 104-105.

⁴Claude Lévi-Strauss, *From Honey to Ashes*, trans. John and Doreen Weightman (New York: Harper & Row, 1973), p. 296.

⁵Ibid., p. 270.

⁶Quoted by Heidegger in "What Are Poets For?", *Poetry, Language, Thought,* p. 130. Heidegger's italics.

⁷See Heidegger, "What Are Poets For?", p. 138.

⁸Quoted by Mary Ann Caws in *The Presence of René Char* (Princeton: Princeton University Press, 1976), p. 313.

⁹See Mary Ann Caws's discussion of this text and of poetry as perfume in *Presence*, pp. 323-324.

CHAPTER 6:

¹Gayatri Charkravorty Spivak, *Translator's Preface* to Jacques Derrida's *Of Grammatology* (Baltimore: Johns Hopkins University Press, 1976), p. xvii.

²Private conversation with Char, June, 1977.

³See Heidegger, "What Are Poets For?", especially pp. 116 ff.

⁴Ezra Pound, "The Flame," *A Comprehensive Anthology of American Poetry*, ed. Conrad Aiken (New York: Modern Library, 1944), p. 320.

⁵Heidegger, "Origin of the Work of Art," p. 47.

⁶Private conversation with Char, March, 1972.

CONCLUSION

¹See Mary Ann Caws, *The Presence of René Char*, p. 317.

[2]See the discussion by Grévisse of the *passé composé* [section 721] in *Le bon usage*, 9th ed. (Belgium: Editions Duculot, 1969), pp. 673–74.

[3]Heidegger, "What Are Poets For?", p. 94.

SELECTED
BIBLIOGRAPHY

Works by René Char:

Place of publication is Paris unless otherwise stated.

Les Cloches sur le coeur. Editions Le Rouge et Le Noir, 1928.

Arsenal. Privately printed, 1929.

Le Tombeau des Secrets. (imprimerie Larguier) Nîmes, 1930.

Ralentir travaux (in collaboration with Breton and Eluard). Editions surréalistes, 1930.

Artine. Editions surréalistes, 1930.

L'Action de la justice est éteinte. Editions surréalistes, 1931.

Le Marteau sans maître. José Corti, 1934.

Placard pour un chemin des écoliers. G.L.M., 1937.

Dehors la nuit est gouvernée. G.L.M., 1938.

Seuls demeurent. Gallimard, 1945.

Feuillets d'Hypnos. Gallimard, 1946.

Le Poème pulvérisé. Editions Fontaine, 1946.

Fureur et mystère (collected edition). Gallimard, 1948.

Le Soleil des eaux. Librairie Matarasso, 1949.

Les Matinaux. Gallimard, 1950.

Art bref, suivi de Premières alluvions. G.L.M., 1950.

A une sérénité crispée. Gallimard, 1951.

La Paroi et la prairie. G.L.M., 1952.

Le Rempart de brindilles. Louis Broder, 1953.

A la santé du serpent. G.L.M., 1954.

Recherche de la base et du sommet. Gallimard, 1955, followed by *Pauvreté et privilège* (collected edition). Gallimard, 1955.

Les Compagnons dans le jardin. Louis Broder, 1956.

Poèmes et prose choisis. Gallimard, 1957.

L'Inclémence lointaine. Pierre Berès, 1961.

La Parole en archipel. Gallimard, 1962.

Lettera amorosa. Gallimard, 1963.

Commune présence. Gallimard, 1964.

Retour amont. G.L.M., 1965.

Les Transparents. Alès: P.A.B., 1967.

Trois Coups sous les arbres, Théâtre saisonnier (collected edition). Gallimard, 1967.

Dans la pluie giboyeuse. Gallimard, 1968.

L'Effroi la joie. Jean Hugues, 1971.

Le Nu perdu. Gallimard, 1972.

La Nuit talismanique. Skira, 1972.

Le Monde de l'art n'est pas le monde du pardon. Maeght, 1975.

Aromates chasseurs. Gallimard, 1975.

Chants de la Balandrane. Gallimard, 1977.

Fenêtres dormantes et porte sur le toit. Gallimard, 1979.

Principal translations into English:

Hypnos Waking. Translated by Jackson Mathews, with William Carlos Williams, Richard Wilbur, William Jay Smith, Barbara Howe, W.S. Merwin and James Wright. New York: Random House, 1956.

Leaves of Hypnos. Translated by Cid Corman. New York: Grossman, 1975.

Poems of René Char. Translated and annotated by Mary Ann Caws and Jonathan Griffin. Princeton: Princeton University Press, 1976.

Critical works on René Char:

Berger, Pierre. *René Char.* Paris: Seghers, 1951.

Blanchot, Maurice. "René Char." In *La Part du feu.* Paris: Gallimard, 1949.

———. "René Char et la pensée du neutre." In *L'Entretien infini.* Paris: Gallimard, 1969.

Blin, Georges. "Préface" to *Commune présence* by René Char. Paris: Gallimard, 1964.

Caws, Mary Ann. *The Presence of René Char.* Princeton: Princeton University Press, 1976.

———. *René Char.* Boston: Twayne, 1977.

Dupin, Jacques. "Préface" to *Le Monde de l'art n'est pas le monde du pardon* by René Char. Paris: Maeght, 1975.

Guerre, Pierre. *René Char.* Paris: Seghers, 1961.

La Charité, Virginia A. *The Poetics and the Poetry of René Char.* Chapel Hill: University of North Carolina Press, 1968.

Lawler, James. *René Char: The Myth and the Poem.* Princeton: Princeton University Press, 1978.

Mounin, Georges. *Avez-vous lu Char?* Paris: Gallimard, 1947.

———. *La Communication poétique précédé de Avez-vous lu Char?* Paris: Gallimard, 1969.

Rau, Greta. *René Char ou la poésie accrue.* Paris: Corti, 1957.

Richard, Jean-Pierre. "René Char," in *Onze Études sur la poésie moderne.* Paris: Le Seuil, 1964.

"René Char," Special Issue of the review *L'Arc.* Aix-en-Provence, 1963.

"René Char," Special Issue of the review *L'Herne*. Paris, 1971.

"Hommage à René Char," Special Issue of the review *Liberté*. Montreal, July-August, 1968.

"René Char," Special Issue of the review *World Literature Today*. Norman, Oklahoma, Summer 1977.

INDEX